IT´S NOT MAGIC,
IT´S CUSTOMER EXPERIENCE STRATEGY

IT´S NOT MAGIC, IT´S CUSTOMER EXPERIENCE STRATEGY

A STEP-BY-STEP GUIDE TO CREATING UNFORGETTABLE EXPERIENCES FOR YOUR CLIENTS AND BOOSTING COMPANY PROFITS

by
CARLOS CORREA RODRÍGUEZ

IT´S NOT MAGIC, IT´S CUSTOMER EXPERIENCE STRATEGY

Original Title: El poder de la experiencia del cliente

© 2020, Carlos Correa Rodríguez Primera edición, Madrid 2020

First English edition, Madrid 2022

Cover design: Contracorriente Layout: Contracorriente

ISBN: 9798831863574

*Dedicated to Claudia and Alejandra,
the two most beautiful experiences of my life.*

Index

Introduction: 7

Chapter 1: For Sale 9

Two Months Later 11

At Home 15

Boston 19

Chapter 2: Emotions 23

Chapter 3: Intelligent Management Of Emotions 35

Chapter 4: Experiences And Their Management. 43

Chapter 5: Money And Income 55

Chapter 6: Knowing And Understanding The Client 63

Chapter 7: Designing Experiences For Your Buyer Persona . . 89

First Example: Veterinary Clinic 101

Second Example: Nut-Psy-Spo Center: Triple Effect 105

Chapter 8: The Senses And Experience 113

Chapter 9: People Who Look After People 127

Chapter 10: Measure, Measure And Measure 143

Chapter 11: One Year Later 149

References: 153

Introduction:

Tragedies

For many years I have observed the same sad statistics. Some 95% of new companies go under within the ten years. The vast majority, over 80%, close during the first year. This is a terrible tragedy. Countless dreams, hours of dedication and vast sums of money evaporate, leaving entrepreneurs broke, broken and uncertain about how to move forward with their lives.

In many cases failure is caused by the lack of a clear business strategy, offering clients "more of the same", products or services they don't want to buy or are too similar to the rest, business plans based on no more than a hunch, a momentary flash of inspiration or a perceived opportunity. Then, inevitably, reality sets in.

My contribution

In this book I will explain a very powerful method that will help you truly differentiate your company. The technique is all about managing the experience of your clients, based on the simple fact that we no longer want to buy products or services. We want to buy experiences. Experiences that bring us joy, that surprise us, that make life easier, that help us enjoy those special moments that life has to offer. The better the experience you offer, the better your clients will speak of your company and the more new clients they will bring.

Step by step

In this book you will find a detailed guide to applying the strategy of Customer Experience Management, set out in clear straight-forward language. We will go step by step, explaining the different stages for successful implementation in your company.

I have selected the most useful and practical tools that I have applied as a consultant for small, medium and large companies for over twenty years and that you can apply to your company immediately.

Straight talk

I won't bore you with long, tedious academic explanations you will find in the kind of articles I had to wade through when researching my doctoral thesis on customer experience and customer loyalty. I'll get straight to the point. I'll tell you what works, what I've learned from my experience as a consultant looking into the eyes of an entrepreneur, helping them transform their company. I have been at this for years and now I want to share what I've learned with you. If you apply it to your business, believe me, you will see a substantial change in your favor.

Talking about you

I will give examples of companies like yours. I won't talk about companies like Disney or Starbucks, Apple or Inditex. Although they may be instructive, they are far from the reality of your business. I will talk about 99.8% of businesses, the ones that generate 74% of employment: small and medium sized companies.

The time is now

The moment is now. Tomorrow is too late. Your clients are crying out for you to seduce and surprise them. They would love to talk about their experience with your company. Do you hear them? This strategy will also bring financial benefits and create significant barriers for your competitors.

Ready to get started?

CHAPTER 1: FOR SALE

It was a fresh spring morning. The street was very quiet with only the faint buzz of a few cars in the distance. Marcos was blinded for a moment by the early rays of sunshine as he fumbled with his keys to unlock the door of the restaurant. He finally managed it and gazed onto the wide empty dining room. He was enthusiastic but also slightly apprehensive about the challenge he had taken on. He exhaled loudly. The rustic birchwood tables were arranged throughout the room, the white tablecloths giving a warm glow to the space, the bottles precisely arranged on the shelves.

Marcos was a 44 year old businessman who had just bought a restaurant in the center of Madrid. His entrepreneurial, energetic nature meant he was almost constantly dreaming up business ideas. The enthusiasm and passion he brought to all his projects was contagious; his employees admired his cheerful, motivating energy. A tireless worker, Marcos was a born entrepreneur.

He closed his eyes for a moment and imagined the restaurant filled with happy clients, smiling waiters and a buzzing, vibrant atmosphere. He retraced in his mind his experiences from the moment he saw the 'FOR SALE' sign in the window until today, keys in his hand. He was certain that, after securing financing from the bank and investing a large part of his savings, the restaurant would be a great success. Both he and his wife were thrilled with the project. For Marcos and Carmen it was like a dream come true and congratulations poured in when they told everyone they were taking on the restaurant.

IT´S NOT MAGIC, IT´S CUSTOMER EXPERIENCE STRATEGY

But as is so often the case, ambition, drive, dedication and enthusiasm are not enough. To be successful in business one must never forget the Customer Experience Strategy.

Two months later

The alarm went off at 7 AM sharp. Carmen woke quickly, lowered her feet from the bed and made her way to the kitchen, the parquet floor giving a gentle creak at every step. She pulled back a chair and sat as Marco served her a coffee with brown sugar followed by some whole-grain toast with the extra virgin olive oil Marcos' mother had brought back from her holiday in Andalucia.

Carmen noticed a troubled look on his face.

"You don't look very well. Did you sleep alright?"

Marcos was silent and took a sip of coffee. "Not great. I'm worried about the restaurant." Marcos paused, a blank look on his face, before continuing:

"I thought the clients would be more faithful. The previous owner ran the place for almost 25 years. I guess I was wrong. There's a lot of turnover. Not many repeat customers."

Marcos sipped his coffee as he tried to organize the thoughts in his head.

"I've only been running it for a few weeks but I think it's time to draw some conclusions. What do you think, sweetie? he asked with a touch of vulnerability.

Marcos always liked to know his wife's opinion and point of view. They had invested a large part of the family savings in the project and it was giving him a lot more headaches than expected.

"I suppose you'll just have to see what's going wrong. Find out why customers don't repeat and make changes until you find the right formula. I'm sure it will all turn out fine, Marcos. You of all people can make it work" she said.

Carmen worked as a psychologist in the human resources department of a well-known supermarket chain that had been growing a lot in recent years. She tried to help Marcos any way she could in this new business venture. It was a project they were both very excited about, although Marcos was managing it because of his experience in business.

"The training center of the supermarket is setting up a project for a new management strategy for the company." Carmen paused to stir her coffee, cooling it down. "My boss told me it's about putting the client at the center of the organization."

"I don't understand what ´putting the client at the center´ means" Marcos said, with a gesture of confusion.

"I'm not so sure either. It has something to do with making the client feel important and the center of attention when they go shopping in our supermarkets." Carmen got up and put her coffee cup in the dishwasher. "Knowing what they like, what they don't like, making sure they have a good experience when they come to our supermarkets or when they buy something online. Our general manager is saying this is a revolutionary management system."

"Well, sure. Your company can do those kinds of things because they have lots of money to invest" Marcos remarked out loud.

"Actually, Marcos, I think the reverse is true."

"I don't get it."

"I mean that the company does well because it does these kinds of things, these initiatives and innovations."

"Oh! I'm running late!" he said suddenly, surprised at how quickly time had passed.

Marcos had a quick shower and got ready to go to the market. He had to pick up some fresh produce for the restaurant.

While he drove to the market, he began musing on how to improve the monthly figures of the restaurant. His overheads in personnel, rent, supplies, loans, etc. were high and, although he had resources from other businesses these were beginning to run short. The pressure was on. He'd put a lot of the family savings into the restaurant, savings that were supposed to go towards the kids' education.

He'd invested in new furniture, upgraded the ovens and installed modern refrigerators; he'd also changed part of the menu and even so, he rarely had repeat customers. He didn't understand why. "Maybe I should lower my prices" he thought. His mind wandered until a beep from the car behind brought him back to reality. The light had changed. He raised his hand in apology and drove across the intersection, finding a parking space directly in front of the market. Normally it was very difficult to park.

"My lucky day" he told himself as he quickly jumped out of the car and went in to place his daily order for the restaurant.

Carmen had called and left a voice message on his WhatsApp.

"Honey, I forgot to tell you, I'll be home late. My boss asked me to visit a few supermarkets, incognito! It'll be fun. I'll tell you later."

Marcos thought that his wife's company did a lot of strange things that he didn't quite understand.

Once he had placed his order he went to the restaurant, greeted the staff and gave them a few optimistic words of encouragement for the day. Marcos was a very enthusiastic person. He always thought he did well in business because of his positive nature and vitality. In the office, sitting in a brown leather chair with white stitching, he took out a notebook and blue Pilot pen. He began to think. Marcos liked to think with pen and paper, turning over his ideas using mental maps. It helped him consider options and reach conclusions, rather than covering the same ground over and over without getting anywhere.

Marcos was worried. His other businesses, although they had their problems, had all gone well. The restaurant was a romantic idea both he and his wife had dreamed of for years. But now he was in trouble. He didn't know how to deal with the problem of building a more or less stable customer base.

"Why don't they repeat? What am I doing wrong? Is it the food? The staff? Are my competitors doing something different?" He was trapped in a cycle of self-doubt and didn't know how to get out of it. His face and hands were sweaty, his eyes watery. He closed his notebook and went to the dining room. His iPhone showed the time as 3:15. The dining room was half full and it was unlikely there would be more customers. Another frustrating day.

At home

After a long day, Marcos arrived home despondent, without an ounce of energy.

"Hi honey. How was your day?"

"Well. Doing the best I can" he said glumly. "But how were your supermarket spy games?" he asked, trying to lighten his mood.

"Very interesting. We had to watch the customers' shopping habits and see how the staff interacted with them. The truth is I'm a bit confused why the general manager and my boss are so secretive. Apparently, they want to completely revolutionize the traditional business model of the supermarket sector."

"Change the model? But everything has already been invented in the supermarket business" Marco remarked skeptically.

"You'd think. But my boss asked if I could put in more hours to co-manage the project with some marketing consultants the company has hired from the United States".

Marcos sat watching Carmen with attention.

"She said my background in psychology makes me the ideal person to lead the project. She even proposed I find someone to help out around the house with the kids while the project is going on."

"You're excited?" Marcos asked with a smile.

"Very" Carmen admitted, feeling that she was discovering a whole new world for herself, one that combined business management and her beloved psychology profession.

Actually, Carmen felt slightly guilty about her enthusiasm. She knew the restaurant was giving him trouble and, while there had been problems with business in the past, this seemed more serious.

Marcos was very energetic and enthusiastic. A go-getter. A problem solver. He preferred to talk of challenges rather than problems, but he was beginning to think the restaurant was testing him to the limit of his abilities.

Carmen returned to the kitchen and saw Marcos browsing through the manual she had left on the table. The acronym C.E.M. was emblazoned on the cover in large letters.

"It's the manual of the changes they're planning to make in the company.

"What's it about?" Marcos asked, intrigued.

"I'm not exactly sure, yet. It's a kind of management philosophy that I have to do some training in. My boss says I need to know it inside out for the transformation to be a success. We want to implement it in all our supermarkets and all the new ones opening from now on.

"The company is betting on you" Marcos said optimistically.

"Yes." Carmen agreed, "it's a big responsibility, My boss and the general manager said we have to interview some customers of the pilot supermarket to see if they like the new model, to find out what they like, and especially, what they don't like,"

"How are you going to implement the new model in all the supermarkets in the country?" Marcos asked, interested but also slightly worried about how Carmen's new company project would affect their lives.

"I'll have to train all the supermarket managers and middle managers too; giving them presential and online training" she replied enthusiastically.

"What about everybody else? Do they get training?" Marcos asked.

"Yes. But for them the training is more specific, especially for those dealing directly with the clients" Carmen explained. "To implement the new management model I'll have to do some training too. At a business school. Just over a week."

"Sounds great. Where? Here in Madrid?

"Not exactly" Carmen replied, not sure how to tell him she would be away for over a week.

Since they'd gotten married they had never been apart. They were always together.

"A bit further. In Boston" she confessed, with a touch nervousness in her voice.

"My wife's going to school in Boston! Like a high-powered executive! Congratulations honey!" Marcos exclaimed, hugging her with happiness.

"When does it start?" he asked.

"My flight leaves tomorrow. They haven't given me any time to make any arrangements. The business school called my boss to say there was an opening and she signed me up without even asking."

Carmen was surprised by the way her husband received the news. She knew he was proud of her and supported her in everything she did, but she wasn't sure how he would react to having to deal with all the logistics, the kids, the homework, meals, etc, etc. And Carmen also knew that the restaurant was keeping him awake at night and constantly on his mind during the day, obsessing about how to turn the restaurant around.

IT´S NOT MAGIC, IT´S CUSTOMER EXPERIENCE STRATEGY

Boston

Carmen arrived at Logan International Airport slightly dazed by her trip. She asked the taxi driver to take her to Lower Allston Street in Cambridge. As she gazed out at the passing landscape from the window of the yellow Ford she had to pinch herself to make sure it wasn't all a dream. She knew that moment would be the start of a priceless learning experience in her life. The taxi stopped at the entrance to the business school where Professor Belt was waiting to greet her.

"Buenos días, Carmen!" he said in perfect Spanish "I'm Professor Belt. How was your flight?" he asked with a friendly smile.

"Buenos días Professor Belt. It was fine, thanks. How lovely the campus is. I can't wait to learn about customer experience management to use in my company" she said enthusiastically. "By the way, where did you learn to speak Spanish so well?" she asked surprised.

"Well. I've had a Spanish teacher for 20 years" Belt answered with a laugh.

Realizing that Carmen hadn't caught his joke, Belt gave a fuller explanation.

"My wife is Spanish. I met her during a research project in Spain years ago."

"Where is she from? If you don't mind me asking" Carmen asked.

"From Sevilla."

"It's a beautiful city. Although summers are very hot" she said making a gesture as if waving a fan.

"And you, Carmen?"

"Madrid."

"I love Madrid. I often go there for conferences. Well, getting down to business. Did you have a chance to read the C.E.M. manual?"

"Yes. But it's written in really technical language. I couldn't really get into it."

"Don't worry. Here we'll break it all down so even a five year old can understand it" laughed the professor, "By the way, what is your academic background?"

"I'm a psychologist", Carmen answered sheepishly, as if apologizing for not having a business background.

"Fantastic! Did you know that customer experience management has a lot to do with psychology?"

Carmen felt relieved to hear this observation from the professor.

"In fact, two of the greatest figures in customer experience management are psychologists. Doctor Bernd H. Schmitt was one of the pioneers of concept of experiential marketing that we'll study in the course and Doctor Daniel Kahneman, who won the Nobel prize for economics in 2002."

"I thought they were both psychologists?" Carmen asked.

"Correct."

"But, I don't understand, you said Dr. Daniel Kahneman won the Nobel prize for economics in 2002."

"That's true. But he's a psychologist. Not an economist, as many people think. He made a very interesting contribution to economics: the so-called prospect theory. Basically, his research showed that people don't make decisions based only on rational or economic criteria. He signaled a key factor in decision-making: emotions."

Belt was clearly a born teacher. It seemed he was about to begin giving class there at the door of the business school.

Carmen felt reassured to hear the course was not for experts and that everything would be fully explained step by step. She was also pleased to know there would be an element of psychology. She had wanted to be a psychologist since she was a child. At the age of just 14 she began practicing with her younger sister Ana. When Ana said she was sad Carmen gave her advice, telling her to sing, to smile more or keep a diary to write about the good things in her life.

When she was still very young Carmen read the famous book by Wayne Dyer, Your Erroneous Zones, that led her to study psychology at university.

After the friendly chat with Professor Belt, Carmen made her way to the residence hall where she would be staying during the course. There she settled in and prepared for the first class.

IT´S NOT MAGIC, IT´S CUSTOMER EXPERIENCE STRATEGY

CHAPTER 2: EMOTIONS

It was a very special day. It was the start of the training program on a subject so innovative that it would revolutionize the business world. The method they were going to learn would impact thousands of organizations and millions of clients around the world, enabling companies to outperform all real or potential competitors. It was 9:00 in the morning. The students from all around the world were in their seats. They were nervous and enthusiastic to learn. Professor Martin waited without saying a word as the students took out their notebooks provided by the business school. The more tech-savvy students used their iPads and laptops. The classroom was small, in keeping with the exclusive nature of the course, and arranged in the form of an amphitheater. At the back were two enormous windows from floor to ceiling that gave onto a beautiful garden and the scent of the flowers seemed to almost penetrate the glass.

"Good morning. I am Professor Martin" he announced, while writing vigorously on the green chalkboard on the wall. "Welcome to the course on Customer Experience Management (C.E.M.)."

The professor went to his desk and dropped the chalk into a wooden box. He looked at the students with a welcoming smile.

"I sincerely hope you enjoy the course, learn and above all, apply the method you will learn during this training program." After a brief pause, he continued "I give you my word that, if you do, you will give a 180° turn to your organization and your balance sheet.

After this introduction and asking each student their name and background and what they expected from the course, the professor raised the first key issue of this business philosophy: EMOTIONS.

Professor Martin began by saying that some believed that there was no place for emotion in the world of business. That emotions were more suited to the world of art, theatre or cinema. However, what had to be remembered was that, regardless of the sector where the students were working, they all had one thing in common: THE CLIENT.

Clients, continued the professor, putting special emphasis on the word, were flesh and blood human being with feelings and emotions. This was both obvious and something that businesses easily forgot. As a demonstration, the professor proposed an exercise to identify the relative importance of the rational and the emotional in making purchases, for example, a handbag, a watch or a bottle of wine. Professor Martin gave the students two minutes to write the results in their notebooks.

"Time!", he called, pointing to his classic Rolex watch.

The student stopped writing. The professor asked the students for their answers, approaching their desks for a closer look and adjusting his glasses. On seeing the answers he raised his eyebrows in surprise, a gesture that did not go unnoticed. He took a moment to make a mathematical calculation of the results and returned to his desk to take up the piece of chalk to write the results on the board: "60% rational and 40% emotional."

"Are you sure these results correspond to reality?" he asked with a smile and a certain touch of irony.

There was only silence. In his experience the professor knew the students would be reluctant to share their opinions in the first class.

The professor took advantage of the exercise to introduce students to the research of Dr. Zaltman, member of the executive committee of the Mind Brain Behavior Program at Harvard University.

"Dr. Zaltman's research found that 95% of our purchasing decisions are unconscious; that is, decisions are taken based on emotions."

The professor paused, watching the class for a few seconds, as if wanting to allow this fact to sink into the minds of the students.

After the pause, he returned to the subject of emotions. To make it even clearer, he gave the students an example, saying that each of us had an experience of buying a product, of feeling better when the person attending us received us with a smile, when the place we bought it from was clean and well lit, furnished in a certain style. If we had any doubts about using the product, we were happy if the employee took their time to explain it to us in a friendly way. Also, when paying, we appreciated that the clerk helped us put the product in a bag and said "have a good day" when we left. Certainly, the next time we needed to buy the same type of product we would unconsciously return to the same place where we had been treated well. Simply put, where we had experienced positive emotions.

The professor then gave an example of an experience of negative emotions. This time in a digital context, to demonstrate that emotion management was important in all interactions with the client, both in traditional settings and online. He used the example of the monthly shop many families made in the supermarket.

"Ok class, how many of your buy food online?"

Four of the ten raised their hands.

"40%. Not bad. I predict that online purchasing will increase exponentially in the next few years."

The professor continued with an example of a family that usually shopped online because they didn't have time to go to the supermarket. They began at the website of a supermarket they saw advertised on a billboard as they drove home. When they did, they found the website was obsolete, the navigation slow and difficult. There was a customer service hotline with no answer. The family spent an average of around $550 a month on food. Of course, the supermarket had now lost this forever by generating negative emotions such as anger, frustration, anxiety and indignation.

"Can you imagine how this terrible emotion management impacts the bottom line of the supermarket?"

The professor made a simple calculation on the board, driving the point home in the minds of the students.

"Imagine that the supermarket had only 200 customers wanting to shop online and they all had the same negative experience as the example."

The professor wrote his calculations on the board:

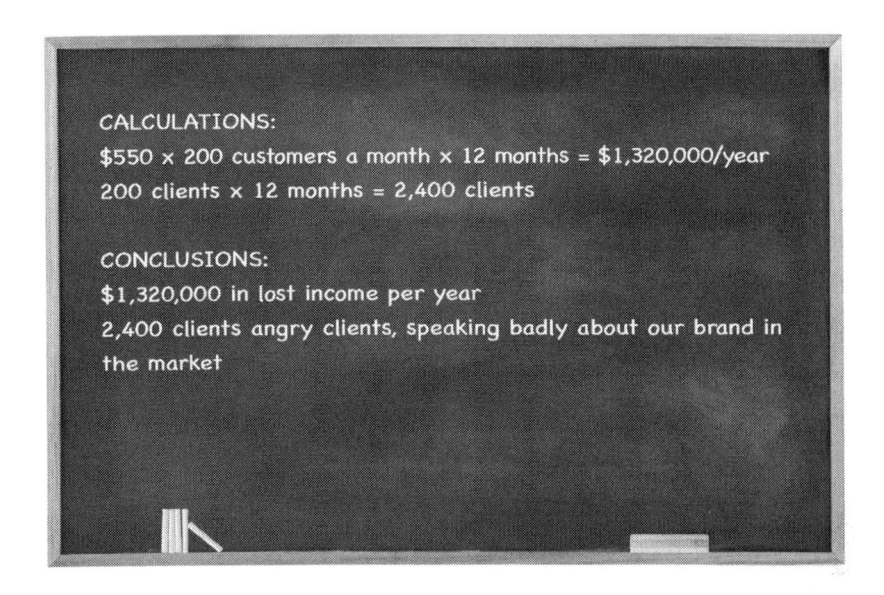

```
CALCULATIONS:
$550 x 200 customers a month x 12 months = $1,320,000/year
200 clients x 12 months = 2,400 clients

CONCLUSIONS:
$1,320,000 in lost income per year
2,400 clients angry clients, speaking badly about our brand in the market
```

He wiped some chalk residue from his hand with a white handkerchief. Leaning against the desk, the professor told the students it was essential to classify the type of emotions that could be generated in the interactions between client and company. He also underlined the importance of identifying which emotions were prevalent in each interaction and referred to the classification by Professor Paul Ekman, a pioneer in the study of the six basic emotions and their facial expressions.

Professor Martin opened a PowerPoint slide on the screen:

NEGATIVE EMOTIONS:

Anger: This is caused when a person experiences frustration. Anger is the result of a perceived threat to one's physical safety, self-image or self-esteem. Excessive anger can even lead to angina, a heart attack, gastrointestinal disorders and other serious health problems.

Disgust: This is an acute aversion or repugnance towards something perceived as highly disagreeable. It can also be produced by vividly imagining such a thing.

Fear: This emotion is highly important to human evolution and survival. Thanks to this emotion, early humans were very careful before leaving their caves, fearful of being eaten by a predator. Fear is a negative emotional state that humans seek to avoid or escape from. Excessive fear can lead to a state of panic.

Sadness: This is a significant drop in the normal mood of a person, caused by feelings of loss or sorrow. It is characterized by a significant decrease in cognitive activity, that is, how an individual perceives reality and behavior. It may range from mind disappointment to extreme feelings of grief and despair.

POSITIVE EMOTIONS:

Enjoyment: This emotion arises when we perceive something as benefiting our life, the achievement of specific objectives, etc. Equally, it can be produced by the mitigation of pain or discomfort, when we achieve a desired goal, or even through aesthetic experience. For example, when we arrive at a hotel and it is better than anticipated, has a huge pool or the staff are very friendly and helpful.

Surprise: This is a very powerful emotion is the world of experiential marketing. It is produced by the unexpected, the novel or unplanned. It is also caused by a happy discrepancy between expectations and reality. To return to the example of a hotel, when checking in at a 4-star hotel only to be told there is a problem with my room and being upgraded to a suite with views of the sea. Hence the surprise and contrast between what was expected and reality.

Many students took notes while others, after asking for permission, took a picture of the image on the screen.

Professor Martin explained that, years later, Ekam created an expanded list of emotions, building on these 6 basic emotions. To clarify, he showed another diagram on the screen.

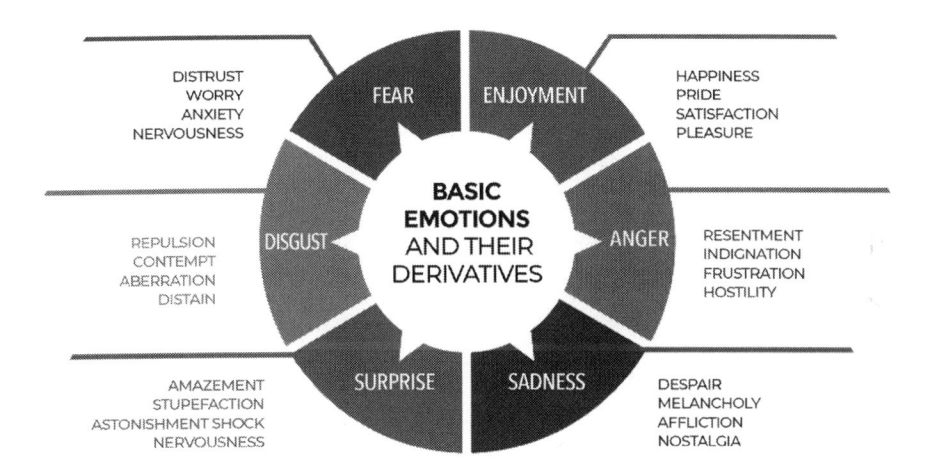

BASIC EMOTIONS AND THEIR DERIVATIVES

- **FEAR**: DISTRUST, WORRY, ANXIETY, NERVOUSNESS
- **ENJOYMENT**: HAPPINESS, PRIDE, SATISFACTION, PLEASURE
- **DISGUST**: REPULSION, CONTEMPT, ABERRATION, DISTAIN
- **ANGER**: RESENTMENT, INDIGNATION, FRUSTRATION, HOSTILITY
- **SURPRISE**: AMAZEMENT, STUPEFACTION, ASTONISHMENT, SHOCK, NERVOUSNESS
- **SADNESS**: DESPAIR, MELANCHOLY, AFFLICTION, NOSTALGIA

The professor called the class to attention. He spoke in a slow and emphatic way while writing on the board:

«People always have an emotional response when they interact with brands. These must be designed beforehand. Never left to chance»

"What happens if we do not control the emotions provoked by our brand?" the professor asked.

He answered his own question saying:

"We run the risk, as in the example with the supermarket, of losing money and reputation in the market. And maybe even leading to the company going under."

Professor Martin signaled a student who had raised his hand.

Peter was the financial director of an important chain of restaurants on the West coast. He wanted to share his personal experience. His company had sent him to the training program because they believed that the success of the customer experience management program depended on all employees sharing the same philosophy, not only those who had direct contact with customers. All departments should be guided by the program, and so they had sent him even though he was in the finance department.

Professor Martin was happily surprised by the vision of Peter's company. He noted that this philosophy required that all company personnel company must be involved, especially the top management. Everyone must be focused on generating positive emotions.

"A company can do a great job serving their clients but any inappropriate experience with someone from some other department, for example, the technical or finance department, can ruin all the good work done by those in direct contact with the client. Don't forget that the chain of experience breaks at the weakest emotion."

Professor Martin wanted to illustrate another perspective of emotions in the world of business. He spoke of the Nobel prize winner Daniel Kahneman, who claimed that humans experience thousands of emotions every day but we don't generally share them because this is frowned upon in our culture. He centered his research on decision-making and found that it could be extrapolated to purchasing decisions that combined economics and psychology. He called this behavioral economics. Kahneman undertook to explain the thought patterns for decision-making when purchasing a product or service.

"Depending on the degree to which a product or service impacts our lives, there is a greater dispute between the rational and the emotional. In this line, Kahneman concluded that human beings take decisions from two perspectives." The professor turned to his Mac and started the projection:

System 1 or Implicit: This is principally a system of decision-making where the emotional plays a greater role; decisions are taken quickly, intuitively and automatically and is most prevalent in our daily routines. Some examples are what pet food to buy, going to the cinema, taking our child to the doctor, etc. This system avoids profound rational thinking or expending energy in considering alternative choices.

System 2 or Explicit: Here there is a greater rational element. Decision-making is slower, calculated and reflective. It's more time consuming but also more reliable and precise. As it is not automatic, we expend more energy and so it's more taxing or uncomfortable. Examples are the choice of hospital for a serious operation, applying for a business loan, choosing a university for our children, etc.

When making decisions, although the two systems are inherently in opposition, they are interconnected and implicit in the decision-making process. All in all, we know that System 1 has more influence on our decisions.

Related to this, Dr. López Rosetti affirmed that we are not rational beings but emotional beings who reason. He coined the phrase:

«The heart decides and reason justifies»

"That's why we must make the effort to produce positive emotions, to allow System 2 to "justify" System 1; that our company generates better experiences than our competitors. Only in this way will decisions be in our favor.

Professor Martin moved to the center of the classroom, explaining that strategic management of emotions was a form of competing within any industry and was an essential factor to be taken into account.

***

Carmen gathered up her things, thinking she should organize her notes. She wanted to have her ideas as clear as possible to make them useful to her company. She remembered what Professor Martin had said at the beginning of the course: "I sincerely hope you enjoy the course, learn and above all, apply in your companies the method you will learn during this training program." Applying it was the important thing, she told herself.

Carmen began outlining in her mind how to plan the training program, first for managers and then the rest of the employees. She was dedicated to her company. They had committed to her, sending her on an exclusive and very expensive training course. She didn't want to let them down.

She left the building and made her way to the residence halls where she was staying during the course. On the way, her thoughts returned to Marcos, the restaurant and the organization of the kids at home. Carmen quickened her pace; she was eager to have a Skype call with her husband and the different time zones made it complicated.

She arrived at the residence hall. It was a neutral, functional, with grey carpeting. Down the hall she spotted a row of vending machines next to the elevators. She bought herself a salad and a Coca Cola Light and went up to her room, holding the salad, drink and handbag as best she could while using the magnetic key card to open the door. She pulled out her laptop and as it started up, she took off her shoes and gave a sigh of relief.

"Hi honey!" said Carmen on seeing Marcos' face on the screen.

"Hi sweety! How was your trip? Your first day of class? It's all pretty intense!"

"Yes. It's been an exhausting day but really interesting" adding after a short pause "how are the kids?"

"In bed."

The six-hour time difference had slipped her mind.

"And how are you, Marcos?"

"Well, you know. A bit lost about what to do with the restaurant" he answered, trying to hide his discouragement.

"I'm learning things about management that, at the moment, seem pretty basic but really interesting. They really known what they're talking about."

Carmen stroked her chin thoughtfully, gazing into space. Suddenly her face lit up.

"Honey, what do you think if I send you emails with the most important ideas of each class? Maybe that can help us with the restaurant."

"That's a fantastic idea" Marcos answered, sensing a ray of sunshine on the horizon.

Marcos needed some fresh, new ideas. He was worn down, blocked. Any new ideas would be more than welcome.

"Honey, I'll send you an email while I'm having dinner. Lots of kisses to the kids. I love you.

"I love you too" Marcos answered, moving the cursor towards the red button to hang up.

IT'S NOT MAGIC, IT'S CUSTOMER EXPERIENCE STRATEGY

From: Carmen@greenmail.com

To: Marcos@greenmail.com

Subject: **EMOTIONS**

Hi again, honey! I'm writing about the main ideas of the class today

They taught me that 95% of purchasing decisions were based on emotions. Maybe you should consider the emotional response of the customers of the restaurant. Do they leave happy?

Another key point is that the emotional response we want to produce should be designed beforehand. For example, when the customer arrives at the restaurant, are they welcomed with a smile? Are the waiters attentive? Maybe we should come up with a little protocol on how to treat and serve the customers.

Lastly, it's essential that you, as the boss, are 100% dedicated and involved. This is super important, Marcos. If you don't take it seriously, how can you expect your employees to do so. See how important it is? You must focus on generating positive emotions and not only when customers arrive at the restaurant but before, when they're on the website, when they call by phone, etc. By the way, you should check the website, maybe it needs updating with some nice pictures, showing opening hours and with a good reservation system, etc.

Well, honey. I'm going to bed. I'm dead tired! I love you.

Carmen

CHAPTER 3:
INTELLIGENT MANAGEMENT OF EMOTIONS

Today was the second day of class. At 9:00 all the students were in the classroom, eager to continue their training course. Professor Martin went over the key ideas from the previous class and then moved on to an equally important aspect of experiences management: the human factor and emotions. Professor Martin gave the students a similar exercise to that of the previous day. He asked an open question to get them thinking.

"We know that activating positive emotions is very important when dealing with clients" said the professor as he walked to the center of the classroom. "Now, we will look at emotions from another perspective. We'll start as we did yesterday, with an open question."

"In the successes of your lives in general, both personal and professional, what would you say is the balance of the emotional and the rational?"

This time he only gave the students one minute to answer. They began writing down their answers in their notebooks. The professor looked at the responses of each student, coming up with an approximate average. The majority gave 50% to the rational and 50% to the emotional.

Professor Martin looked silently at the students for a few seconds and then continued his lecture by mentioning Professor Daniel Goleman whose research showed that the intellectual accounted for between 10% and 20% of personal success.

In 1995, Goleman coined the concept of 'emotional intelligence', which he defined as the capacity to understand one's own feelings and those of others, and the ability to manage them.

Professor Martin added another definition. He clicked on his Mac and projected a PowerPoint slide

> **EMOTIONAL INTELLIGENCE:**
>
> «The capacity to understand one's own feelings and those of others, to motivate and manage relations with others appropriately»
>
> «Capacity for self-reflection: Identifying one's own emotions and regulating them appropriately»
>
> Dr. Goleman

He clarified that our rational faculties helped to resolve difficult situations, such as making calculations to build a bridge, creating a vaccine for a specific illness, etc. The weighting of 10% to 20% was far from irrelevant, and no one would seriously doubt the importance of rational thought and reasoning. But Goleman affirmed that it was necessary to go beyond the intellect for success in life and he called this the intelligence of the emotions or emotional intelligence.

Martin emphasized that human beings are social beings and the key to successful socialization was a high level of emotional intelligence.

"Are your clients social beings or, on the contrary, are they merely statistics, numbers without feelings or emotions?" he asked, hammering the concept into the students' minds.

The professor insisted that in the business world this skill was the key to dealing with clients, understanding them and generating positive experiences.

The professor then showed the 5 basic principles of emotional intelligence, highlighting the importance that employees have these skills.

Emotional self-knowledge: This is not new. Over two thousand years ago, Socrates coined the famous phrase "know thyself". This is the foundation of emotional intelligence, that is, being aware of your own emotions when they arise. If we are not aware of them, we cannot manage them effectively. For example, Peter is a waiter in a Boston restaurant. Today he is working and it's the anniversary of his mother's death. Thanks to Peter's emotional self-knowledge we will be able to realize he is sad because of the memory of his mother.

Self-control: To manage your own feelings that give rise to emotions of any kind. This serves to filter and mitigate the appearance of negative emotions, such as anger, hate or fear. This ability is fundamental for interpersonal relations. Returning to the example of Peter, he is working and thanks to his self-control he can manage his sadness, being friendly and attentive in dealing with customers. Thus, if a client is rude, he will exercise his self-control to solve the client's problem and/or request, and not take things personally.

Self-motivation: Emotions tend to drive action. When you are aware of your emotions or even can produce them, you can use them to act and achieve your objectives; for example, control your impulsiveness, improve every day, oblige yourself to smile more, be more friendly, pay more attention to clients, etc.

Empathy: The ability, either innate or acquired, to understand the emotions of others. In other words, to put yourself in the shoes of another. This ability is fundamental for those having contact with clients.

Creating relationships: When you learn or perfect this skill you acquire the capacity to create and maintain positive interpersonal and commercial relationships, for example with your clients. This means your brand will be stronger, creating not only a rational but also an emotional connection. Returning to the example of Peter the waiter: he knows what I like, he takes care to ensure my family and I are comfortable and he's happy to see us. All of this makes me feel good about the restaurant.

The professor offered a series of facts that corroborated his earlier talk. According to the World Economic Forum (WEF), emotional intelligence was one of the 10 most in demand skills in 2020. Also, a recent study found that 71% of those surveyed valued emotional intelligence above all other attributes.

"It is important for the success of your businesses that you internalize the idea that customer experience management in your companies means having a solid team of professionals trained in Emotional Intelligence."

The professor pointed out that in order to implement an experiences management project it was essential that company employees receive training in emotional intelligence. He reflected on the importance of recruiting personnel with certain skills so that, when they received the appropriate training, the learning process is more effective and profound.

"If you hire people with high levels of emotional intelligence it will be easier to orient them towards experience management" said the professor as he paced the classroom floor.

"I always share this phrase with the hundreds of professionals who come through our classrooms each year, and I would like you to keep it in your mind:

«If my employees have poor emotional intelligence and treat my clients badly, they are no longer my salespeople, they are salespeople for my competition»

With this sentence the professor aimed to show that if employees dealt with clients poorly, they would go to the competition. At the same time, he emphasized that every moment of contact with the client was a golden opportunity to generate positive emotions, and that this was possible only with employees with high levels of emotional intelligence.

"To conclude the class, I will give you this phrase from Roosevelt:

«The most important single ingredient in the formula of success is knowing how to get along with people»

The professor brought the class to a close until the following day. He stood at the door of the classroom saying his goodbyes to each of the students by name. Many were surprised by this feat of memory.

IT´S NOT MAGIC, IT´S CUSTOMER EXPERIENCE STRATEGY

From: Carmen@greenmail.com

To: Marcos@greenmail.com

Subject: THE INTELLIGENT MANAGEMENT OF EMOTIONS

Hi Honey:

I hope you are feeling better and the kids are behaving.

In today's class we dealt with something that is very important for any business, but especially for a restaurant like ours. It's called Emotional Intelligence. It's all about managing emotions, both of the employees and the clients.

Remember telling me about how friendly and thoughtful the barbers are where you get your hair cut? They wish you happy birthday, know what you like or that time you complained about having to wait and they sent you a surprise gift voucher for a free haircut for you and the kids? And for some reason, even though they're on the other side of the city, you have been going there every month for years. And since the free haircut for the kids you've been taking them for years too. That's it. That's intelligent emotion management. When you complained they knew how to turn it into an opportunity to surprise you. They earned your loyalty as a client, and they also picked up two more clients: the kids!

On the other hand, I also learned the opposite scenario. If an employee treats a client poorly, they will go to the competition.

Have you watched how the waiters interact with customers at the restaurant? Are they friendly and polite? Are they attentive or are they chatting among themselves?

Honey, I think it's very important that you work on these issues.

I'll write again tomorrow! And remember that Marta has a dentist appointment tomorrow. Don't forget!

Lots of kisses for you and the kids

Carmen

IT´S NOT MAGIC, IT´S CUSTOMER EXPERIENCE STRATEGY

CHAPTER 4: EXPERIENCES AND THEIR MANAGEMENT

The professor arrived at 8:50, greeting the students as they came in. Some carried cups of coffee that they dropped in the waste basket beside the classroom door. Through the windows, timid morning rays of sunshine gave a warm light to the room.

"Good morning class! I hope you all slept well" began the professor in a cheerful voice.

By 9:00 all the students were seated and ready for the class. The professor took off his jacket, leaving it hanging on the hook beside the door. He moved across the polished wooden floor into the center of the room and there he began.

"In previous classes we spoke about the concept of emotions and emotional intelligence in business. Today we will delve a little deeper into the concept of experiences and their management."

Beginning with the concept of experience, Professor Martin first gave the dictionary definitions of the word. He noted that one of these included: "the fact of having felt or witnessed something". Others referred to "lived circumstances or events". He went on to tell the class that the study of experiences and emotions was framed within the field of experiential and sensorial marketing. Another, more business-oriented definition was provided by the researchers Pine and Gilmore, who understood experience as "events that involve individuals in a personal way", noting that "products are tangible, services are intangible, and experiences are memorable."

The class learned that experiential marketing dealt with defining a set of actions aimed at provoking a series of specific emotions in a profile of client or specific user when they interact with a brand.

"The objective is to create long term relationships with the target client of the brand by generating emotions that lead to unforgettable experiences" Professor Martin clarified.

He then referenced the global expert in marketing Philip Kotler, who claimed that brands no longer compete for market share but for what he called "heart share". Kotler wanted to emphasize the importance of emotion and experience in the attachment clients felt to brands. This was a source of competitive advantage.

> *«The brands that can generate unforgettable experiences for their clients will be stronger and more competitive».*

The professor introduced the students to the true purpose of customer experience management, emphasizing the idea of creating a clear and tangible DIFFERENTIATION from competitors in the minds of target clients and the public.

He argued that differentiation was the way for brands, products or services to stand apart in a positive way from the competition. This attribute could be technical, for example a mobile phone that has a voice activated search feature. It may also be an emotional attribute, for example, the brand of your phone represents values of innovation, data security, status, etc.

"A question" said Professor Martin. "What attributes provide long-term differentiation?"

Martin explained that technical attributes were most easily imitated by competitors, except in the case of patented features. And once the patent expires, competitive advantage vanishes. He went on to mention that differentiation had an emotional basis, where imitation is more difficult. This is part of the essence and culture of a company itself.

"Ideally, these aspects are combined: the technical or rational with the emotional" explained Martin.

The professor gave an example of a restaurant that innovated in their menu, incorporating new dishes suggested by loyal clients and naming them as "recommended by Daniel or Teresa". This gave their menu certain dynamism and created a space for the surprise factor. Similarly, it is important to use tools for emotional differentiation, such as giving clients an outstanding service, having pleasant music in the evenings or even putting the kitchen in the center of the restaurant where clients can see the chefs prepare their meals, as if giving a performance for the diners.

"All of these tools for emotional differentiation must be aimed at a specific target audience" he noted. "Obviously, not everyone likes the same things."

The professor mentioned another key concept: POSITIONING, which is nothing other than the place a brand occupies in the mind and heart of the target client in relation to competitors. Normally, this is the most salient attribute. For example, the positioning of the brand Volvo is related with the idea of safety.

Martin expanded on the concept of experience management, telling the students that Customer Experience Management (C.E.M.) was a strategy to design and manage the interactions of a client with a company, generating unforgettable experiences.

At this point, Professor Martin wanted to show students the strategic vision of Schmitt on the management of experiences.

"Schmitt understood management as a sales strategy based on the added-value provided by transforming a product into an experience.

The professor paused for a moment to loosen his tie.

He explained that Customer Experience Management was a strategy to consolidate a competitive advantage. The purpose is to increase customer loyalty, recurrent purchases and to encourage clients and users to recommend the brand, among other aspects. All of which had a positive impact on company revenues and profits.

When a client interacts with a company, they experience a series of perceptions. These perceptions lead the client to make a final verdict on whether the interaction is good or bad. Hence, proper management consists in not leaving these perceptions to chance; they must be planned, defined and articulated to ensure they are excellent.

Martin noted that when a client enjoyed a memorable experience, this resulted in attraction and attachment to the brand, leading to greater loyalty and people sharing their experiences with friends, family and work colleagues.

They might even make positive comments on social media, encouraging others to have a similar experience. This was the final step; that the client gives glowing reviews and so becomes a promoter and evangelist of the brand.

In designing experiences we must understand what is important to the client. There is no point investing in highly aesthetic or sophisticated design when the client does their shopping online and will never visit our space.

"Now I will give you a summary of the most important ideas about the implementation in the company of Customer Experience Management (C.E.M.)" the professor announced, projecting a new slide on the screen:

KEY IDEAS ON CUSTOMER EXPERIENCE MANAGEMENT

1. A strategy to compete in the market
2. Company management and owners must lead implementation
3. Greater profitability and competitive strength can be achieved by offering unforgettable experiences to our target client
4. Pursue customer loyalty and engagement over the long term
5. Focus on a specific profile or target client
6. Make the client a seller of the virtues of your brand in their circle and online ('word-of-mouth')
7. Leave nothing to chance
8. Employee training and education is the key to success

9. All the experiences should be homogenous, not depending on a single or specific contact person

10. Operate in the emotional and rational space of the client

11. Establishing protocols for interaction is essential

12. Measuring the impact of actions is essential

13. The entire process must be excellent from start to finish
14 Constant innovation will make our company more competitive

«*Customer Experience Management is not a fad. It is a way to compete that looks for profitability by keeping clients happy and loyal, promoting our brand. This involves a substantial cultural change*».

"Any questions?! The professor asked, turning towards the classroom.

"Yes. I have a question." said Carmen, raising her hand. "In my company, in the supermarket sector, we sell top brands like Nestlé, Häagen-Dazs, Pepsi, Coca-Cola, etc. Do you mean that having leading brands is not so important?"

The professor took advantage of the question to explain that meeting basic needs, that is, selling the brands customers want, does not produce satisfaction since they consider this something basic. In fact, the opposite is true. Not having them produces dissatisfaction.

On the other hand, meeting the emotional, unexpected needs does produce differentiation from the competition.

To make the concept even clearer, the professor gave an example of a local pharmacy. This example could be extrapolated to any other sector. He reminded the students that the size of the company or business was unimportant, but what mattered was the strategic vision and innovative drive of the management.

"Imagine you go into a pharmacy to buy aspirin. The pharmacy is poorly lit, the floor is not particularly clean, there shelves are disorganized, the clerk at the till is on the phone to a friend talking about what a good time they had on the weekend. They barely acknowledge you when you pay, hand you the change and give a feeble "bye". You spent $1 on a pack of aspirin.

The professor paused to write "Pharmacy B" on the board.

"Now let's look at Pharmacy B. You want to buy the same pack of aspirin. The pharmacy is clean and well-lit, the furnishings are modern, the clerk looks you in the eye with a sincere smile, says hello, asks you what you need, you answer you have a headache and the pharmacist agrees with your choice in a friendly way, puts your purchase in a paper bag and wishes you a good day.

"In both establishments you paid exactly the same amount. If you had to buy the same thing again or even recommend a pharmacy in the future, which one would it be?"

"Pharmacy B" answered Carmen instantly.

The professor noted that the client's experience was much more positive in Pharmacy B than A, and that even if the product was more expensive in Pharmacy B the majority of client would be willing to pay more for a better purchasing experience.

> *«The majority of consumers are willing to pay more for a better purchasing experience»*

FRIENDLINESS

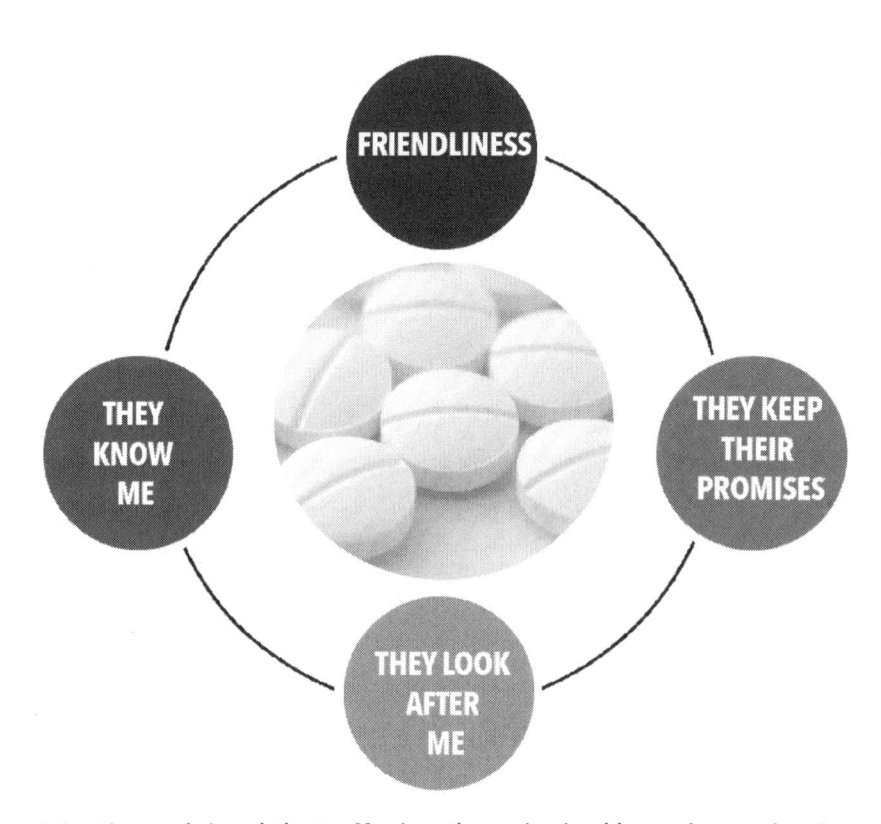

THEY KNOW ME

THEY KEEP THEIR PROMISES

THEY LOOK AFTER ME

Martin explained that offering the principal brands was basic, not a differentiating factor because the majority of competitors offered the same products. What's more, almost all consumers go to one place or another to buy a product not for the product itself but for the experience. It's not a product being sold but an experience and the emotions that surround the product.

Martin mentioned that there were companies where if you asked executives or owners what they did, they would answer they sold food, cut hair or installed alarm systems. However, in companies which put the client at the center rather than the product would answer they sold culinary experiences (restaurant), they wanted their clients to feel attractive (hairdresser) or they wanted their clients to feel safe (alarm systems).

PRODUCT-CENTRIC STRATEGY	CUSTOMER-CENTRIC STRATEGY
WE SELL FOOD	WE OFFER CULINARY EXPERIENCES
WE CUT HAIR	WE WANT OUR CLIENTS TO FEEL ATTRACTIVE
WE SELL ALARM SYSTEMS	WE WANT OUR CLIENTS TO FEEL SAFE

"We have to change the paradigm. Every time clients interact with your company the objective must be to activate their positive emotions. We no longer sell products or services; we are sellers of EXPERIENCES."

IT´S NOT MAGIC, IT´S CUSTOMER EXPERIENCE STRATEGY

From: Carmen@greenmail com

To: Marcos@greenmail com

Subject: EXPERIENCES AND THEIR MANAGEMENT

Hi Honey:

Today's class was long and exhausting but very interesting. Professor Martin is great. He's really passionate about his subject and it shows.

We talked more about a company being stronger and more competitive when its able to generate memorable experiences for its clients. C.E.M. is a way to compete. They idea is to make clients happy and profitable, that they recommend and promoter us in their personal life.

We also saw that the same experiences do not work for every client. They have to be focused on a specific profile. From now on we shouldn't focus on selling menus or food, but gastronomic experiences. I mean that the experiences and emotions created around a meal are very important, almost as important as the product itself.

Do you remember when we went to Córdoba for my birthday? They treated us wonderfully. When we checked into the hotel it was super quick with the app, no line-ups, the staff knew our names and were always smiling, the room was beautiful, and they also surprised us with a bottle of champagne and chocolates, with a note from the hotel manager wishing me a "Happy Birthday" on behalf of the entire staff. Remember it was such as lovely dining room, with a pianist playing soft, romantic music in the background. And remember we went down to the parking garage and the car was sparkling clean.

I know the hotel wasn't cheap but the experience was well worth it. In fact, six of my friends have gone to the same hotel because of our recommendation. Remember? Well that's what people are looking for these days. Customer experience. Surprise and seduce the client and they will recommend you to all their friends and on social media.

Honey, you have to analyze what aspects you can change to give clients an excellent experience, from the moment they walk in, to the moment they leave. Just like the hotel in Córdoba. In class, we learned that the majority of clients are willing to pay more for a better experience. And so I think lowering prices is not a good strategy. It would be better to improve the experience, don't you think?

Well honey. I hope all this information is useful.

Take care and lots of hugs and kisses to the kids

Carmen

IT´S NOT MAGIC, IT´S CUSTOMER EXPERIENCE STRATEGY

CHAPTER 5:
MONEY AND INCOME

The professor arrived in the classroom at the scheduled time. Everyone was struck by the fact he wore a baseball cap with a $100 bill stamped on the front.

"Today we're going to put on the money hat!", he said raising his voice. "Every time you think about investing in experience management, I want you to think about return on investment. I don't want you to forget that when a company, large or small, decides to implement experience management, it does so to make more money, to be stronger and more competitive, and to protect itself from competitors who base their strategy on offering lower prices.

Professor Martin took off the cap and carefully placed it on a lectern to the left of the podium. He wanted to give it a place of importance.

"Let's not forget that the purpose of any company is none other than to make money. I am proposing to earn it through this innovative experience management strategy."

IT´S NOT MAGIC, IT´S CUSTOMER EXPERIENCE STRATEGY

Smoothing his hair, he walked to the center of the classroom, while recalling the conclusions from the previous class that showed customers were willing to pay more for a better shopping experience.

Professor Martin remarked on the conclusions of the researchers Pine and Gilmore who claimed that when companies strategically organized memorable events for their customers, the product or service took a back seat. In these cases, the customer perceived a higher value, called experience. In this way, the company could charge clients for transformation, that is, the client pays not only for the tangible, but also for the intangible associated experience.

"For example, if I go to a paint shop to buy four 5 kg cans to paint my son's bedroom and I am served by someone who explains how to apply it, gives me a tip on how to put it on the wall better, gives me a demonstration right there and then on how to use the product correctly and happily advises me on decoration, obviously I will be delighted when I leave the store since I only expected to buy paint (a tangible) and really what I acquired was a remarkable experience."

The professor strode to the central aisle that divided the classroom in two and explained that what Pine and Gilmore meant was that when you sold not only paint, but offered an experience, you could charge the customer for the paint and for the experience. To sum up, you will be more profitable if you also sell experiences instead of just a product or service.

The professor wanted to share with the students a list of reasons why a company should seriously consider the idea of implementing customer experience management as a competitive tool.

"These arguments will also be useful in case you have to convince your bosses", Martin said, walking to his table to hit the key on his laptop and project a slide.

HOW DO I MAKE MORE WITH C.E.M.?

More satisfied customers: The customer will perceive your company is making an effort to offer more value. People like that and are attracted to the brand.

Customer attachment to the brand: If we improve the customer experience with the brand, they will stay with it, wanting more different and special experiences.

Repeat purchase: It's only human to go back to where you were treated well. When you invest in customer experience, it shows on the balance sheet.

Low abandonment rate: Customers feel more loyalty and their level of abandonment will be much lower. More than 80% of customers who abandon their suppliers do so because of poor customer experience.

Increased sales: Loyal customers tell their family, friends and acquaintances about their experience. They act as promoters. Some 62% of customers buy because of references from friends and family.

Increased sales per customer: With good experiences purchases per customer will be greater.

The price is less relevant: This, often ruinous, factor can be offset by good experiences. When the experience has more weight in a client's perception, the price has less. Studies shown that over 82% of customers would be willing to pay more to ensure a better customer experience.

You will spend less on advertising in the different media: From now on your clients will be your billboards, your most valuable salesforce.

Increased profitability: Companies that focus on customer experience increased their profitability by more than 22%; while those with worse evaluation saw their profitability drop by more than 45%.

"I repeat," Martin continued, "To achieve the points in the slide, it is essential to take customer experience management very seriously and put the emphasis on it.

"Well class, thank you for your attention during these modules. It has been a real pleasure. In the next class you are going to meet Professor Barker, who will introduce you to the main actor in this wonderful production," Professor Martin said, raising his hands with a slightly priestly gesture, as if referring to the transcendental. "Get some rest. And good luck to you all."

The students politely said their goodbyes as they closed their laptops, put away their notes and the C.E.M. manual.

CUSTOMER EXPERIENCE MANAGEMENT

GOOD MANAGEMENT 👍

1. MORE SATISFIED CUSTOMERS
2. MORE LONG-TERM CUSTOMERS
3. MORE REPEAT CUSTOMERS
4. LOWER RATES OF ABANDONMENT
5. INCREASED SALES
6. HIGHER AVERAGE PURCHASE
7. PRICE IS LESS IMPORTANT
8. LOWER ADVERTISING COSTS
9. HIGHER PROFITS +22%

👎 BAD MANAGEMENT

1. DISSATISFIED CUSTOMERS
2. HIGHER CUSTOMER ROTATION
3. FEWER REPEAT CUSTOMERS
4. HIGHER RATES OF ABANDONMENT
5. LOWER SALES
6. LOWER AVERAGE PURCHASE
7. PRICE IS VERY IMPORTANT
8. HIGHER ADVERTISING COSTS
9. LOWER PROFITS -45%

IT´S NOT MAGIC, IT´S CUSTOMER EXPERIENCE STRATEGY

From: Carmen@greenmail.com

To: Marcos@greenmail.com

Subject: MONEY AND INCOME

Hi honey:

Today we finished the last module with Professor Martin. He's been with us for the last few days and I was a bit sad to see him go.

This time we talked about money. He told us that almost 90% of companies are basing their strategy on generating better customer experiences. We should also use this strategy to create a stable customer base for the restaurant.

By offering a special experience to our clients, they will come back again and again. This was what worried you most: to have a stable clientele. They'll also talk about their good time at the restaurant and recommend it to their friends. We have to shoot for that, Marcos. Get them to speak highly of us, so we'll have more customers. How? By giving them a better experience, so they have a good time in our restaurant.

Remember when we went to the dentist with Marta for the first time? The first thing we did was to look for references on the Internet. We really liked the comments about how warm and friendly the dentists were with the children. Then, when we took Marta we saw it was true. We've been going there for years, and because of our recommendation to parents in the park, a lot of neighbors have taken their children there too (maybe we should ask the dentist for a commission 😄)

But seriously. The idea is to make money by having our customers fall in love with us. Obviously, we can't forget the basics: the food has to be excellent. On the other hand, the idea of experiences is now a global trend for companies and if we don't do the same the restaurant might even go under. We have to take this issue very seriously and start thinking that we are selling experiences and memories.

I love you, Carmen

IT´S NOT MAGIC, IT´S CUSTOMER EXPERIENCE STRATEGY

CHAPTER 6: KNOWING AND UNDERSTANDING THE CLIENT

"Good morning class! I am Professor Barker. Allow me to start off this beautiful spring morning by sharing with you a professional experience. It was a consultancy that I did some years ago for a company in the fashion industry."

The teacher made a brief pause to capture the attention of the students. He then took off his stone-grey jacket, folded it with care and left it on the back of his armchair. Around 60 years of age, the professor had a serious but charming face and an air of vitality that was both positive and seductive.

"I'm going to present the case of a small company in the fashion sector that franchised its business model. Today it has 250 outlets all over the country. The General Director is named Mateo and he started running a tailoring shop here in Boston 20 years ago."

"Mateo was truly obsessed with knowing his clients. He said that one's manner of dressing was a faithful reflection of one's inner mood, personality and how you relate to others. He spent much of the time of client's visits enquiring, honestly, about their lives, if they had children, where they worked and lived, what their hobbies were, etc. At the same time, on the emotional level, he asked how they felt, if they worried about work, their joys and fears... And so Mateo gathered information on the personal lives of his clients. To be fair, he did this for a perfectly legitimate

IT´S NOT MAGIC, IT´S CUSTOMER EXPERIENCE STRATEGY

purpose: to know and understand his clients and what they wanted, and so be able to offer a suit to meet their tastes, needs and personality."

"This peculiar tailor wrote everything down in a brown leather notebook. On the left-hand side, he wrote down the rational aspects and on the right-hand side, the emotional ones," explained the professor as he moved about the classroom.

Professor Barker told the students that with these notes and the feedback he received, Mateo made sketches he showed to clients to see if it fulfilled them. He didn't ask if the client 'liked' it, but if it 'fulfilled' them. Mateo was looking for a more emotional response instead of offering a simple cotton suit of a certain color.

Mateo had no formal knowledge of experience management, but he did something amazing: he said that he had to 'strive to surprise' his clients because he didn't have the money to advertise. His only marketing was his clients bragging about their suits, and this meant that a lot of his new clients came through recommendation.

"I think that, even if he had had money, he would have put the same passion into his work "Everything comes from the client," he said."

Students took notes in their notebooks and in their electronic devices. They seemed enthusiastic.

The professor carried on with the story. He reached a transcendental point in the life of Mateo and his company. Over the years, Mateo had accumulated hundreds of notebooks with comments on the tastes of his clients.

One weekend while he was organizing his notebooks an idea came to him. As he read over the notes, he realized that a lot of his clients had similar tastes. He created groups based on tastes, socio-cultural profiles, emotional traits, etc. Then for each group he invented a profile that represented that group. For example, "Peter" was the client profile or archetype for a group of businessmen who lived in a certain area, who had family, liked a particular sport, etc. "John" represented a group of university educated professionals who worked for large companies, had small children and shared lifestyles, habits, etc.

Mateo asked his son for help, recently graduated in computer engineering. They designed a software application and fed in all the information collected over the years in the notebooks. When introducing the features of a new client, the software proposed suits tailored to his rational and emotional profile. Mateo's son gave him a lot of ideas. By combining traditional industry with technology, together they developed a successful company based on offering the client what they wanted to buy. And so, an innovative customer experience was generated.

The excited professor took a sip of coffee and resumed his talk.

"The basis of this company is not technology. Technology is only a means to sort data and extract relevant information The basis is the deep knowledge of the client: knowing and understanding the client by putting them at the CENTER of the organization."

The students were totally absorbed and highly motivated by Barker's story. He explained they were going to study the protagonist of experience management: the CLIENT.

He explained that their obligation as leaders or implementers of this management model was to know as much as possible about the client's life, their environment, joys and sorrows, what they liked or disliked, feared, what they felt and did not say, etc.

"How are you going to make a suit, if you don't take the measurements of the client? Similarly, how are you going to design a successful customer experience if you don't know or understand them very well?"

He insisted that, if you did not truly know the client, you ran the risk of designing experiences that were not aligned with their tastes and desires. This was a waste of time and money, leading thousands of companies to ruin every year.

"Knowing and understanding the wishes of clients is the difference between making money or having to shut down. Believe me!" said the professor with his fists clenched for emphasis.

Tool 1: SEGMENTATION

After the pause, Barker began by offering the definition of "Segmentation" given by the American Marketing Association (AMA): "the process of subdividing a market into distinct subsets of customers who have similar needs within the subset, different from other subsets. Each subset could be conceived as a goal that was achieved with a different marketing strategy."

Another definition the professor gave was that by Philip Kotler and Gary Armstrong. According to them, a market segment was "a group of consumers, companies or organizations that responded in a similar way to a certain set of marketing efforts."

"To illustrate the concept more clearly, I will give you an example of mass marketers, such as supermarkets.

"Segments: Singles, marriages without children, marriages with children, vegetarians, savers, gluten-free consumers, lactose-free and their combinations."

The professor explained that clients could be grouped by their needs, concerns, income, way of life and consumption habits.

Once consumer groups were categorized, we could identify new segments by conducting, for example, in-depth interviews with a certain group or segment. If we asked what products they missed in the supermarket and a large number answered: 'petfood', then another segment could be identified to satisfy.

If the research shows that an important segment has pets, it could be a great opportunity to include petfood and pet accessories within the mix of products.

With this, several business objectives were achieved: to provide more value to current customers who have pets, to boost sales, increase the average purchase and ensure customers did not buy from another supermarket that does offer pet products as well as everything else your supermarket offers.

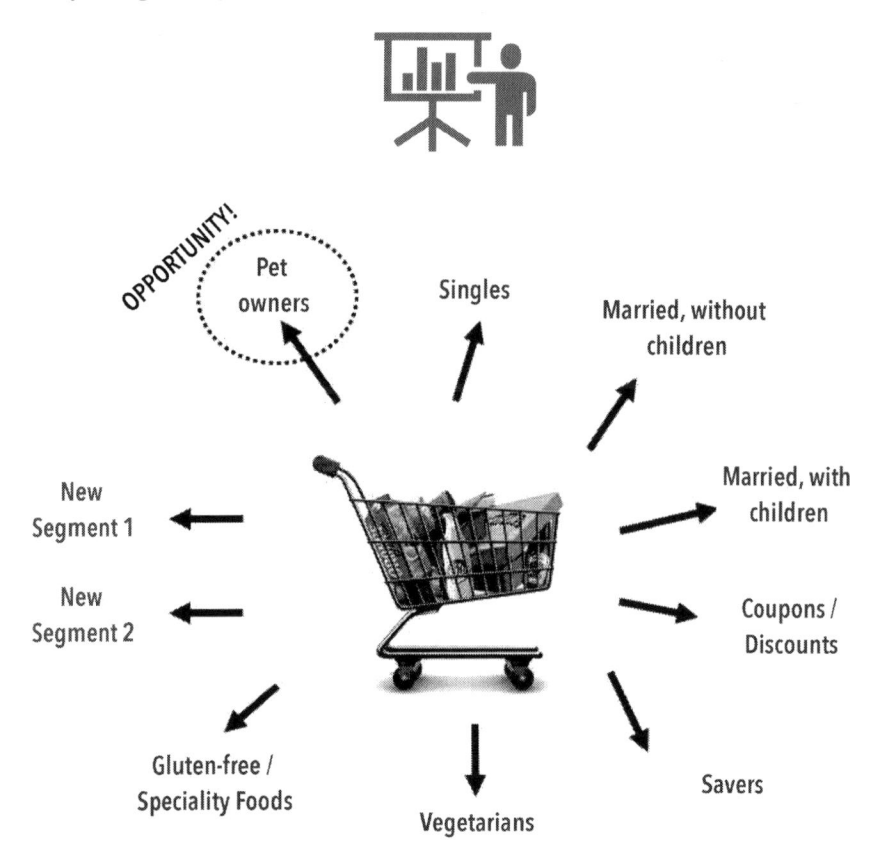

OPPORTUNITY! — Pet owners

- Singles
- Married, without children
- Married, with children
- Coupons / Discounts
- Savers
- Vegetarians
- Gluten-free / Speciality Foods
- New Segment 2
- New Segment 1

The professor repeated that to know what our target client wants it is essential to seek them out and listen. He leaned on the table and rolled up his shirt sleeves.

"Attention class! Seeking out the opinion of the client makes it easier for us to know how they perceive our company, what expectations they have when buying our products or services, what they miss, what they have, what bothers them or what they dislike when buying, and so on."

"This is a key tool to measure the experience of clients with our organization, to correct shortcomings, to identify new and unmet needs, to build loyalty and attract clients with the same profile."

«The client should determine the mix of products or services the company offers. For this, it is essential to hear the voice of the client»

The professor criticized companies that knew the theory but failed to put it into practice. It seemed beyond them to select a representative group of clients within a segment and openly ask them what they liked most about the company, what they liked least, what they loved and what irritated them. He said this step was fundamental to designing unforgettable experiences.

"Segmentation is conducted according to the criteria I will now show you," said the professor, projecting an image on the screen:

1. GEOGRAPHICAL:

Where do they live? This helps us to know if our clients live in a certain area of the city or the country. This geographical knowledge will help us, for example, to do more efficient marketing from an operational point of view and in terms of profitability. By knowing where our clients are using zip codes, it will be easier to focus advertising and commercial actions in that specific area. This way we avoid throwing money away in areas where we won't find our target clients.

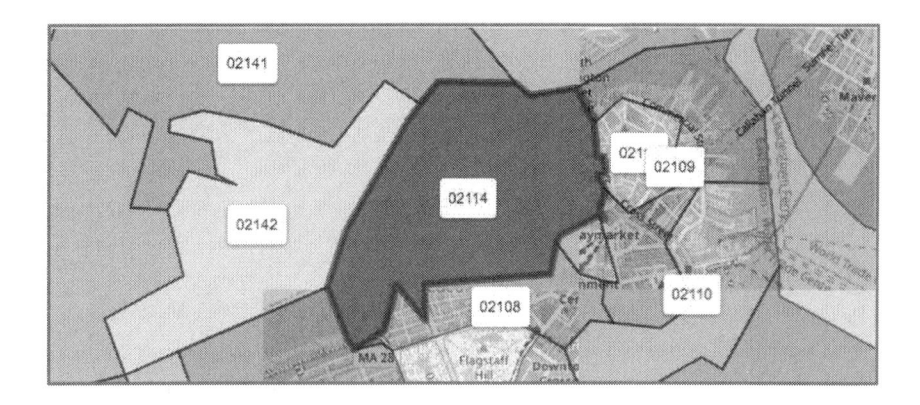

IT´S NOT MAGIC, IT´S CUSTOMER EXPERIENCE STRATEGY

2. DEMOGRAPHICAL:

Age, sex, income, level of education, nationality, race, profession, etc. As before, we find out the average age and gender of those who make purchasing decisions about our products and services. Income is a key variable. Knowing the average salary by zip code provides very useful information about what type of products or services should and should not be advertised.

"One day I walked through a neighborhood of the city whose zip code had a low-income profile. That's why I was surprised to see there a billboard advertising a brand of premium cars. Surely, they did not sell a single car in that district."

3. PSYCHOGRAPHICAL:

In this section we talk about consumption habits, personality and lifestyle, status, daily activities, eating habits, political opinions, sports preferences, culture, values, etc. As you can see, the segmentation variables complement one another.

4. BEHAVIORAL:

How people spend their money, how much they spend on sports, leisure, travel, pets, etc. If they are loyal customers, bargain hunters, etc.

The professor gave the example of a small company which used client segmentation based on the four criteria presented in the Power Point slide.

"We are going to invent a company called Your New Garden. This company belongs to you since gardening is not something I find especially interesting, so you can keep it," Barker said laughing.

"Your company is headquartered here in Boston. It offers garden maintenance services as well as gardening equipment, such as irrigation systems, fertilizers, pesticides, lawn mowers, etc. You want to identify where your target clientele is.

Barker paused and, after taking a look at the students, continued:

"Once we identify where our potential customers live, we will segment them to offer them the specific services and products that each segment needs. We'll focus on two segments that, in theory, may require our services. Let's make an analysis using the segmentation criteria we've just seen. These are the results of our market research:

DEVELOPMENT 1:

Geographical: A housing development of semi-detached houses with gardens of about 50 ft². The zip code of the area is 02126. The average price of homes in the area is between $400,000 and $600,000.

Demographical: Men are usually responsible for contracting gardening services or buying garden accessories such as plants, planting tools, seeds, fertilizers, etc.

Residents are generally couples earning a combined income of between $60,000 and $90,000. The average age is 37 years old with 2 young children. Both spouses generally have a college education and work as skilled professionals in consulting, services, banking, insurance, etc.

Psychographical: These are generally families who like to enjoy being at home, having parties and get-togethers with family and friends. They are environmentally aware and are interested in gardening, especially fruit trees and vegetables for their own consumption. They are savers, planning ahead for the cost of university for their children and the unexpected. They do outdoor sports, such as walking or jogging. They vote for party X.

Behavioral: They spend their money mainly on things for the home, on food, gardening, education, sportswear, the odd evening out, etc.

For this segment of homes with small gardens, where the owners like gardening, the company will offer gardening products and accessories since, according to the research, it is the owners who look after their garden, mow the lawn, etc.

"Continuing with the same model, let's analyze Housing Development 2 in another zip code.

DEVELOPMENT 2

Geographical: A development of individual houses with large gardens of about 1,000 ft^2. The zip code is 02124. Property values in this area average from $1 to $2 million.

Demographical: There is a maintenance service that deals with garden service providers and presents the owners with prices and arranges the services. Residents here are generally couples with an average income of between $400,000 and $600,000. The average age is 47 years old. They may have 2 children at university. Both are university graduates. These are generally entrepreneurs or managers in large companies.

Psychographical: They have an active social life at the country club in the area. They enjoy meeting with friends in the club, play golf, tennis, etc. They like sailing and horse riding. They belong to select social and cultural organizations. They travel to Europe twice a year for holidays. They are savers and investors. They tend to vote for party Y.

And finally,

Behavioral: They spend their money on luxury cars, holidays, boating and horse riding, prestigious universities for their children, etc. They expect exclusive service in the places they visit, such as hotels, restaurants, etc.

IT´S NOT MAGIC, IT´S CUSTOMER EXPERIENCE STRATEGY

SEGMENT	GEOGRAPHIC	DEMOGRAPHICS	PSYCHOGRAPHICAL	BEHAVIORAL
DEVELOPMENT 1	Semi-detached. Zip code: 02126 Boston Garden 50 ft^2 Home: $400,000-600,000	37 years of age 2 children Income: $60,000-90,000 Education: University Occupation: skilled professionals	Home bodies Enjoy family and friends at home Interests: gardening, ecology, Joggers, athletic, urban Values: family, enjoying life Savers Vote for Party X	They spend their money on: Household products Gardening Education Sports Pragmatic
DEVELOPMENT 2	Detached. Zip code: 02124 Boston Garden 1,000 ft^2 Home: $1 – 2 million	47 years of age 3 children at university Income: $400,000-600,000 Education: University Occupation: Business owners / Top management	Bust social life Enjoy family and friends at the Country Club Golf, travel, sailing, horse riding Lifestyle: Family, friends, politics Values: family, enjoying life, business Savers and Investors Vote for Party Y	They spend their money on: Luxury cars Boats Education at top universities Sports, horse riding They enjoy luxury and exclusivity

In this segment, houses with large gardens, the company will offer garden maintenance services, accessories and products since, according to our research, the owners are not responsible for caring for their gardens.

"I hope that this exercise with a small gardening company will make it clear how geographical, demographic, psychographic and behavioral segmentations are combined.

The professor paused for a sip of water and then continued:

"We've talked about where they live, their level of education, how much they make, what and how they buy, etc."

"Don't you feel that something is missing? Hello! I'm customer number 456, I live in the ZIP code 02126 and I earn $75,000. What's missing?

The students noted the lack of any aspects related to emotions. It was clear by their comments that the training was sinking in, giving them new perspectives in seeing the business world and, specifically, the client.

The professor nodded, telling the students that if we wanted to provide our clients with an experience that would touch their hearts, we must first know their heart. That is, their emotions. He also reminded them that clients were flesh and blood human beings with feelings and emotions like everyone else, people who laughed and cried, had good days and bad days, experienced joy and sadness. "That's why, as Professor Martin told you, empathy is the golden key to managing experiences."

"Tomorrow I will give you to another very interesting and useful tool to successfully implement a Customer Experience Management project. This will help you get to know your clients more deeply, especially at an emotional level."

IT´S NOT MAGIC, IT´S CUSTOMER EXPERIENCE STRATEGY

From: Carmen@greenmail.com

To: Marcos@greenmail.com

Subject: TO KNOW AND UNDERSTAND THE CLIENT /Segmentation

Hi Honey!

We just finished today's class I'm very tired, but it's been so worth it.

The professor explained a tool called segmentation, a very useful way to identify the profile of current customers. That way we can focus on the most profitable and so offer them the service they're looking for or really want.

Remember when we bought my Volkswagen Golf? Apart from telling us about all the features of the car, the dealer explained that the Volkswagen group had different brands for different types of clients.

Remember? He said:

Audi: For people of a certain status, the most expensive car of the group, a company cars for managers, etc.

Volkswagen: For those who like to show off their car, with good technology and power.

SEAT: Aimed at younger and adventurous people who want a reliable make.

Škoda: Good technology at the best price, appealing to the usefulness of the product rather than status or prestige, etc.

Well, that's segmentation. To know your customer in order to offer one thing or another. Can you imagine investing in the effort to sell an Audi to someone who earns $15,000 a year and is looking for a practical car? Logically, it will be easier to sell them a Škoda.

What are the restaurant's customers looking for? How many segments do you have? Which are the most interesting and profitable?

Maybe there's an ideal segment from Monday to Friday and a different one for the weekends. In that case, you would have to offer different things, don't you think?

To do the segmentation you would have to know:

Where they live or where they work (for example, are they executives who work in companies nearby and eat there from Monday to Friday or are they people who live in the neighborhood).

Income, age, education, profession, etc. You need to know all this information because if they are single, it makes no sense offering them a meal to celebrate they're kid's birthday on the weekend. This may seem silly, but it's not. The professor told us during the coffee break that thousands of companies all over the world spend millions every year on advertising aimed at the wrong people. We don't want that to happen to our restaurant, do we?

We should get to know their lifestyles, daily routines, values, political opinions, cultural interests, the sports they practice, if they have children, pets, what they spend their money on, etc. All of these are relevant aspects the entrepreneur should take into account.

To begin with, when people go to pay, you could ask them their zip code, if they come because they live nearby or because they work in the area or on a recommendation. It would be interesting to see what type of people go to the restaurant. With their zip code, using existing market studies, you can know their profile in terms of income, lifestyle, education, etc.

IT´S NOT MAGIC, IT´S CUSTOMER EXPERIENCE STRATEGY

Honey, I think we're on the right track!

Go for it!

👍

I miss you

Big kiss to the kids

Carmen

Tool 2: EMPATHY MAP:

Professor Barker arrived in the classroom 15 minutes before the start. He was leaning over his Mac, going over the slides for the class, a look of intense concentration on his face. It was clear he enjoyed his work. When the first student arrived, he looked up and, with a kind gesture, wished him good morning.

When all the students were settled in, he greeted them politely and wished them a good day of learning.

"Good morning class! Today we are going to X-ray the client, get to know them deeply and intimately. We are now going to review the concept of empathy that you studied with Professor Martin."

The professor reminded them that to have empathy, one had to know, in addition to the segmentation criteria, how clients felt, what their fears were, their values, their joys, their sorrows, what motivated them, what held them back, etc. In this way, we could get closer to their emotional core.

"To know the client we will use a second tool called the Empathy Map. This tool was developed by the entrepreneur and consultant Dave Gray.

Professor Barker explained that it was about creating a questionnaire, based on a previous segmentation, of a sample of the clients or kind of clients our company would like to have. This was through a personal interview aiming to know them in more depth, especially in terms of their emotions, feelings and view of life.

"With this information, we will be able to design innovative services that will generate surprising emotional experiences for that specific profile of client."

The professor went on to explain that the idea was to empathize with the client, to know what and how they feel. The tool helped to put a face, eyes and, especially, a HEART to the client and know what truly motivated them.

He recalled that motivation was the prelude to an action. The word *'motivation'* was derived from the Latin *'motivus'* or movement and the suffix *'-tion'* referring to action and effect.

"We will be able to design special experiences for our clients based on hypotheses about their real motivations". At this point, the professor referred to a phrase from the famous businessman Scott David Cook:

> «Empathy is not walking in another's shoes.
> First, you must remove your own»

"The Empathy Map is not about you. It's about getting to know your clients by removing the filter of what you like or dislike."

To demonstrate the usefulness of the tool, the professor returned to the case presented the previous day, this time focusing on Housing Development 1. He selected a sample of 4 representative clients from the segment.

After the in-depth interview, each participant was given an ecological gardening course, valued at $250.

"Remember that this segment, Development 1, includes the profile that enjoy gardening. It's important that the gift is in line with their interests.

The following questions were used to create the Empathy Map:

1. What do you think and feel?
- What motivates them
- Interests, concerns
- What they really care about (but doesn't say)
- Professional, personal ambitions, etc.

2. What does he say and do?
- Behavior in public
- What they say they care about?
- Who they talk to?
- Do they influence anyone?
- Is there a difference between what they say and what they think?

3. What do they see?
- In their environment
- Offers they are exposed to
- Key people in their environment
- Problems or challenges they face

4. What do they hear?
- In their professional environment
- What their family and friends say
- Main influences: friends, boss, parents, etc.
- How do they do it?
- The media they use

5. What frustrates them?
- Frustrations
- Fears or risks they worry about
- Obstacles they face in achieving their goals

6. What motivates them?
- What they really want to achieve
- What is their concept of success
- How are they going to achieve it

To make the example more revealing, Professor Barker projected onto the screen an in-depth interview with one of the participants from the "Development 1" segment.

1. What do they think and feel?
The most important thing in life is family.
I love spending time with friends and the kids at home.
Work is important. I'm always trying to improve.
I worry about the future but I'm optimistic.
You can achieve things with hard work.
You have to prepare for the future.
Stress is a pandemic in the 21st century

2. What do they say and do?
I like to learn gardening techniques to practice at home.
I like my house, my TV and I help out in the kitchen.
I look for clothes and things for the home on Amazon.
I like to enjoy the garden, having a drink after dinner with my wife.
I help my kids with their homework.
I dress formally for work but without being too strict.
I go running almost daily with my kids.

3. What do they see?
A healthy and active family and professional life.
My friends have children and are from my professional life.
Weekends are for spending time with family.
We travel around the country.
I work hard and am valued in my company.

4. What do they hear?
My father was an example of perseverance, values and morals.
My boss is a leader in the business world.
The opinion of my wife and my friends is important.
Sports is necessary for physical and mental health.
We have to care for the natural environment and recycle.
I admire athletes like Usain Bolt.

5. What frustrates them?
I deal with stress at work by doing sports and things around the house.
I'm afraid of losing my job.
I need to be valued in my professional life.
I worry about the health of my family.
I worry about saving for my kids' university education.

6. What motivates them?
Progress in my company. I like a challenge.
I appreciate that my suppliers are well-mannered and polite.
Making more money is important.
Feeling healthy and doing sports with the family.
I love and encourage doing things as a family.
I enjoy my home and enjoy growing fruit and tomatoes as a hobby.

"The principal aim in creating an Empathy Map is to collect relevant psychological information to know and understand the ideal client as much as possible. The information collected will be the basis for creating innovative experiences."

IT´S NOT MAGIC, IT´S CUSTOMER EXPERIENCE STRATEGY

Barker noted that much of the information obtained would have a significant emotional charge. He reminded the students that the main objective of the generation of experiences was to excite and enthrall the client. He explained that Empathy Maps could be used to compile the most relevant and coincident **data** from the participants. This information would form the basis for understanding using a third research tool.

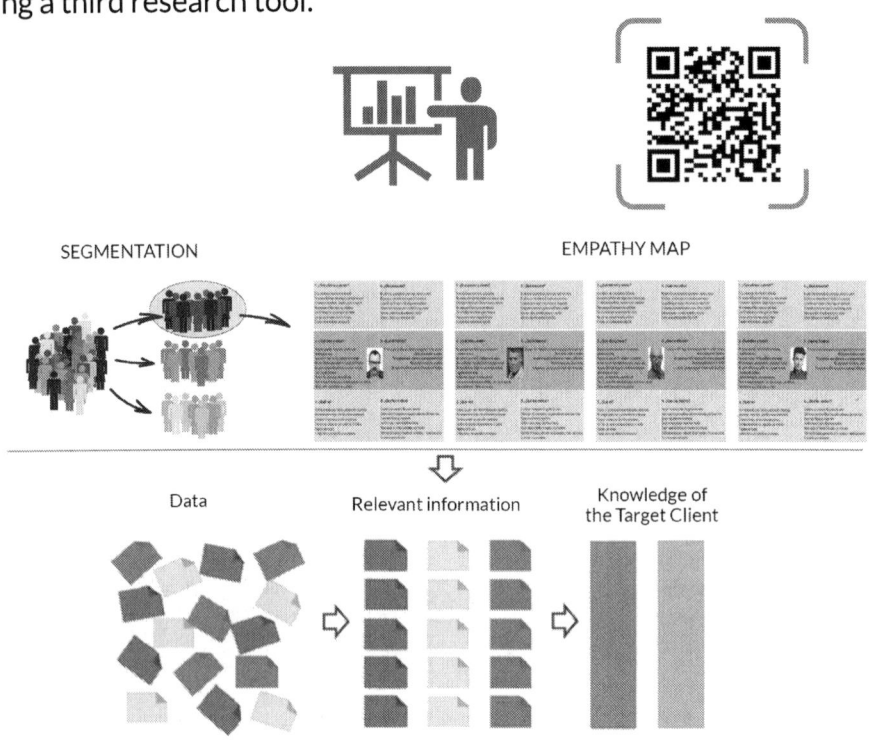

SEGMENTATION   EMPATHY MAP

Data   Relevant information   Knowledge of the Target Client

"The idea is to identify the most special, representative and recurrent information about members of the segment and thus extract key data and have sufficient knowledge of the target client in order to make use of tool number 3, which I will explain to you after the beak.

Tool 3: CLIENT OR BUYER PERSONA

"Ok, class, let's continue with the third step in client knowledge"

The professor explained that after segmentation, and deciding on the most interesting segment for the company, Empathy Maps were made of representatives of that segment The data was then analyzed to extract relevant information that can translated into knowledge, to identify both emotionally and rationally, our BUYER PERSONA.

"The BUYER PERSONA is a fictional character combining most of the emotional and rational attributes of the chosen client segment. In this way, our team can visualize and focused more closely on designing experiences for our BUYER PERSONA, who in turn represents our target clients."

"Creating the BUYER PERSONA is the key to designing the global value package and outlining the customer experience we are going to offer."

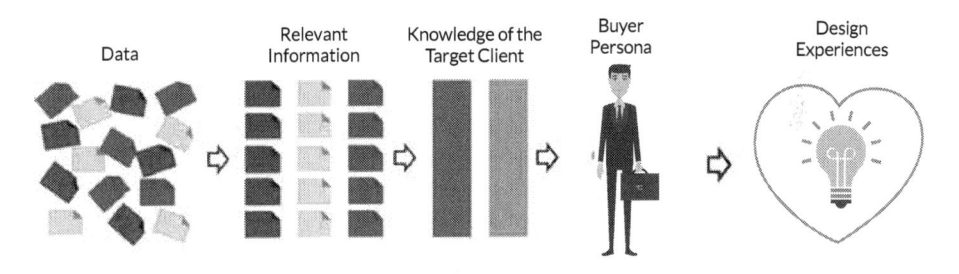

Data ⇨ Relevant Information ⇨ Knowledge of the Target Client ⇨ Buyer Persona ⇨ Design Experiences

"Class, by using these three tools, from **segmentation** to the **Empathy Map** to the **Buyer Persona**, you have all the keys to gain a profound insight into your target client. This will enable you to design and manage the experiences you are going to offer to leave them delighted."

BUYER PERSONA OF HOUSING DEVELOPMENT 1

Daniel is our Buyer Persona. He is a university graduate working in a consulting company. He earns $85,000 a year. He has two children and meets the other profile characteristics of the Housing Development 1.

He enjoys spending time with family, working in the garden, looking after the plants and growing fruit and vegetables. The children sometimes set up a fruit stand outside their home and make a few dollars.

His values include environmental responsibility and ecology, life-long education, charity work and community involvement.

"We have identified the client we want to surprise. We have their emotional and rational profile. In the next class, Professor Jones will instruct you on how to design a beautiful and emotional experience, which your target client will surely enjoy."

Segmentation ⇨ Empathy Map ⇨ Management of data, information and knowledge ⇨ Buyer Persona ⇨ Design experiences

----

From: Carmen@greenmail.com

To: Marcos@greenmail.com

Subject: TO KNOW AND UNDERSTAND YOUR CLIENTE (EMPATHY MAP AND BUYER PESONA)

Hi Honey:

I hope you feel more encouraged with the emails I've been sending you. Today we had our last class with Professor Barker. The truth is that I'm feeling a bit sad. He's someone who really speaks from the heart and that's really inspiring.

Today we saw a couple of very interesting tools. The idea is to identify what kind of clients we have and what kind of clients we want to attract. It's called an Empathy Map. It's the next step from the segmentation tool I told you about in my last email. You have to give this as much importance as you give to the quality of the meat and fish you buy in the market.

Once you have **segmented** your clientele, check their zip codes and what they have in common (if they have a family, are managers who work in offices in the area, business lunches, etc.). Decide if this is the profile you want for the restaurant. If so, you must get to know them emotionally and so be able to offer them an exciting experience that makes them want to come again. This means you have to interview a number of clients from the chosen segment. Tell them it's for an innovation project and if they agree to participate, they will get a free lunch for them and their partner. Believe me, this information is vital for our restaurant. I've attached the questionnaire. It's called an **Empathy Map**.

Once you've done several interviews, you must analyze the data to find the most relevant aspects, especially emotional ones. In this way, you can produce a model client that represents each segment. This model is called the **Buyer Persona**. You can even give them a name. 'Daniel', for example. 'Daniel' symbolizes the emotional and rational profile of your target client, making it easier to **drill down** and find out what 'Daniel' really likes.

It's important to identify what they like, what they feel, what motivates them, their fears and goals in life, and so on. With this, we can have a more in-depth understanding of the different customer profiles and so offer them products that give them a better experience in our restaurant.

Well honey, it's getting late!

We'll speak tomorrow

I love you,

Carmen

CHAPTER 7: DESIGNING EXPERIENCES FOR YOUR BUYER PERSONA

It was 8:45 a.m. The morning was damp although the students were already shielding their eyes from the morning sun as they arrived at the school. The lawns looked neat and trim, and there was a strong smell of freshly cut grass in the air. It was quiet except for the gentle murmur of the students entering through the main door of the building, guarded by four columns of white marble.

Inside the classroom, Professor Jones was waiting. He was a man in his 50's wearing a Navy-blue suit, a white shirt and a matching tie. He was tall and athletic and moved with a certain style on the polished floor while erasing the board.

He went through the attendance list, wishing a good morning to each of the students and introduced himself.

"I'm Professor Jones, a specialist in creating memorable travel experiences, although I never worked in a travel agency," he said smiling. "We will start with a listening. Everyone, please close your eyes."

The class closed their eyes and some exhaled purposefully, ready to engage with the exercise.

The teacher activated the device and a deep, velvety voice began to speak accompanied by a subtle background music.

"Fran is an enthusiastic person. Enjoying life at every moment. He works hard in an insurance company, where he has forged good connections with his clients and among his co-workers. He entered as an intern and in ten years he was already regional director. Today was his wedding anniversary. To surprise his wife, Anna, he went to pick her up at the door of her work with a matte black Harley Davidson and with their bags packed. She loved motorcycles. When Anna walked out the door of the building where she worked, the roar of the motorcycle caught her attention. It was like a black panther. It was Fran, revving the Harley. She couldn't believe it, her mouth wide open with a carmine red smile. Without a word, she ran to him giving him a passionate kiss. She got on the Harley screaming, 'Let's go!'"

The audio ended and the teacher observed that, if we wanted to impress our partner with a ride on a Harley, we needed to choose a route beforehand, the roads to travel, the landscapes to see, the exact time of arrival at a certain place to enjoy an unforgettable sunset, etc. And, where to have dinner. To make the moment special we would need to call the restaurant and book a table with beautiful view. To impress even more, we would promise the waiter a hefty tip to give us extra special treatment.

This trip created a highly emotional experience, loaded with positive feelings. But it also required painstaking planning for each stage to go according to plan. Nothing is left to chance.

"I hope that the example of the trip Fran organized makes it clear that to surprise the client every last detail must be planned."

"Here is a slide showing the customer journey map or, as I like to call it, the Customer Experience Map (CEM):

Designer of the experience: Fran (husband) Client: Anna (wife)

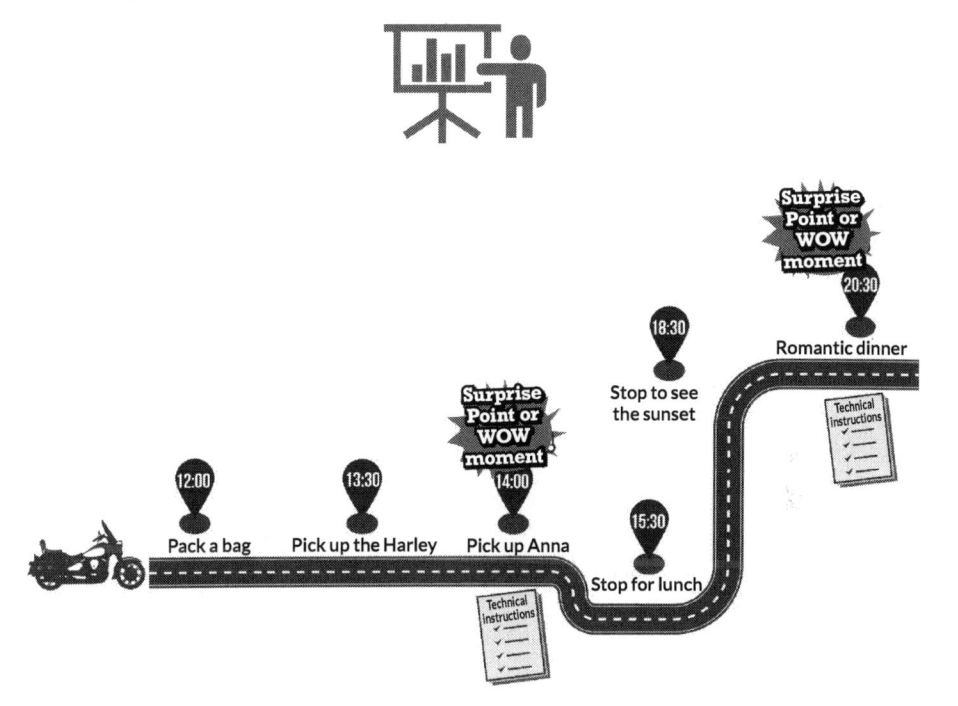

Journey timeline:
- 12:00 — Pack a bag
- 13:30 — Pick up the Harley
- 14:00 — Pick up Anna — *Surprise Point or WOW moment*
- 15:30 — Stop for lunch — Technical instructions
- 18:30 — Stop to see the sunset
- 20:30 — Romantic dinner — *Surprise Point or WOW moment* — Technical instructions

The professor reminded the students that with his colleague Professor Barker they had identified the profile of the ideal customer or Buyer Persona. He also stressed that, thanks to the Empathy Map, they knew they had very similar behavioral and emotional needs.

He paused briefly to take a sip of water from a blue bottle on the desk.

He went on to argue that, once the segment of ideal customers had been identified, for example the most profitable clients, the aim was for them to be repeat customers, that they would be more loyal and promote our brand among their peers, that is, among their friends and acquaintances with the same customer profile.

"This loyalty and free promotion are gained by offering them a unique and well-differentiated experience. Getting our customers to tell others about their experience is strategic and we must focus all our efforts and creativity to achieve it," said the professor raising his voice in emphasis.

Professor Jones went to the coat rack and, excusing himself, removed his Navy blue jacket. The sun was beginning to warm up the classroom. He continued by presenting a tool for customer experience planning.

"The tool is called the Customer Experience Map (CEM). It serves both to evaluate, in an orderly manner, the experience of current clients and to identify areas for improvement and to design innovative experiences that surprise our client or Buyer Persona."

He went on to explain that the Customer Experience Map (CEM) was composed of the different phases of the client's interaction with the company, regardless of whether the interaction was in-person or online as it was applicable to all kinds of sectors and industries.

"I'm going to show you how to create a Customer Experience Map (CEM)" he said, turning to the screen.

1 Identify the stages the buyer goes through. Whether a physical shop, a law firm or any other business, before going to the establishment you will have probably visited the website, Facebook or Instagram profile, LinkedIn (for company-company or B2B) or even other websites where there are comments on their services, etc. This visit to any digital environment would be the first stage.

2 Identify the expectations and objectives of the buyer at each stage. When going to the website maybe they want to see the products for sale, the physical address, the telephone number, etc. Or, in a physical environment, you have the expectation to buy, and not to have to wait in line, to park easily, to receive fast, efficient and friendly service, among others.

3 Identify the reality the customer perceives versus their expectations at each stage and at points of contact (PC): Points of contact are the moments when the buyer interacts with your brand and staff. Here we must find out what the client truly wants. For example, they want to buy in a certain shop and want to park easily but in fact it takes them 35 minutes to find a parking spot. Another may be that a family wants to buy a television and the clerk is unkempt or doesn't make the effort to explain the benefits of the product. This phase is key because it is here where many areas of improvement and possibilities for surprise can be identified.

4 Identify your emotional assessment at each point of contact during each stage: It is important to know what the purchaser FEELS at each point of contact The emotions of each phase can be ranked on a scale: very positive (+2), positive (+1), neutral (0), negative (-1) or very negative (-2). Here you can identify **Surprise Points** at best or **Pain Points** at worst.

5 Propose areas of improvement and innovation, in great detail, at different points of contact in order to surprise the client: l The idea is to create Surprise Points at certain moments of contact.

6 Evaluate your proposals: Once you've identified the points of contact where to surprise the client and proposed ways to create Surprise Points, these must be evaluated. This can be done by asking the opinion of friendly customers or employees in direct contact with customers using surveys, etc. We don't want to design Surprise Points that aren't really surprising or are not perceived as such by the client.

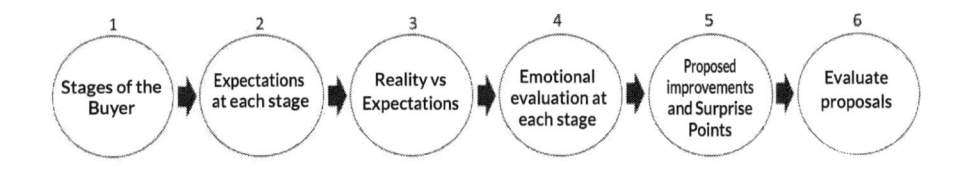

1. Stages of the Buyer → 2. Expectations at each stage → 3. Reality vs Expectations → 4. Emotional evaluation at each stage → 5. Proposed improvements and Surprise Points → 6. Evaluate proposals

PAIN POINTS

The professor wanted to explore the concept of Pain Points in more detail. He explained that these were specific moments when negative emotions were generated, as Professor Martin had discussed in the class on emotions. These emotions could be of different types: anxiety, anger or frustration. Pain Points were especially harmful to the profitability and reputation of the company and it was essential to identify and eliminate them as quickly as possible.

"With this you have to be very careful; you have to be vigilant. I'm going to give you the most agile techniques to identify Pain Points:

- In interviews conducted to design the Empathy Maps
- Focus Group: with a representative group of customers
- In-depth interviews
- Comments on the website and ratings by customers
- Complaints
- Mass customer questionnaires, etc.

SURPRISE POINTS

"Now, we will look at the opposite scenario, that is, Surprise Points or 'Wow' moments," said the professor with a slight air of euphoria as he paced the stage.

Professor Jones went on to comment that:

"Surprise Points or Wow Moments should be designed in a way that the customer fervently wants to tell their experience to friends and acquaintances"

Surprise Points take place when the customer is positively impressed by something unexpected. He clarified that Surprise Points were created, strategically, in stages or at very specific times in the customer experience.

"You should not try to make every stage a 'wow' moment because that would be unreal and unsustainable. But it is very important to design a Surprise Point at the end of the experience since it is usually the moment people most remember afterwards."

The professor went on to say that Surprise Points remain in the memory for a long time and have a big impact on both company revenues, reputation and level of recommendation by customers.

Surprise Points → Positive Emotions → Attachment to the Brand → Positive Actions → Promoter of the Brand

He went explained that Surprise Points had to be planned honestly and sincerely so the client is at the center of the experience and, therefore, feel they are the real protagonists.

"These moments must be simple and fun. Nobody likes complex experiences or that cause stress. And one thing you should never forget is that these experiences are burned not only into the memory, but especially in the heart!" Jones stressed.

CREATING MEMORABLE SURPRISE POINTS:

The professor went on to give some ideas about what aspects should be considered when creating Points of Surprise and how to make them indelible in the memory of the client. He stressed that managing waiting times was very important. Basically, we do not like to wait. He pointed out that younger people, digital natives, want everything immediately and that waiting is a significant pain point. Another important aspect to keep in mind was to customize the service or the product. Professor Jones added that he had recently bought a tie online and when it arrived, he found a handwritten note thanking him for the purchase and hoping he liked the article. He stressed that managing unexpected moments, such as being called by your name, scored points.

"Dale Carnegie said that, for every person, his name is the sweetest and most important sound in any language. You should keep this in mind whenb dealing with a client; call them by their name in a natural and friendly way. But, without overdoing it", he added with a smile.

He explained that surprising the customer did not necessarily have to be expensive. For example, inviting diners to a drink while they waited to be seated in a restaurant, delivering a car freshly washed at a repair shop, giving a child a sugar-free candy when they're with their parents at the pharmacy, having a magician in a toy store to liven up the atmosphere, being friendly, giving a genuine smile, etc.

INNOVATION: THE KEY TO THE STRATEGY

After the break, Professor Jones told the class he wanted to talk about an important ingredient in the design of experiences: innovation. He noted that Surprise Points, if repeated over and over again, unsurprisingly, ceased to be surprising. They had to evolve and be renewed every certain period of time.

"It's important to innovate, to generate new experiences that connect to the real emotions of customers."

The professor explained that innovation required a team of creative people, and that creativity was the first step towards innovation. He noted that the key to creativity was essentially the generation of ideas.

"Creativity is ability to create ideas. These can be new or updates of older ideas. Creativity helps us design new value propositions that can improve people's lives and generate new experiences."

The professor added that, in experience management, innovation should be concentrated on the client. This requires focus, requires tools and requires a clear commitment by management. Training in innovation is essential, for all employees at every level of the company.

Every employee must be aware of the importance of this issue for the company and, furthermore, be given the skills to identify opportunities for innovation in their interaction with customers.

"As you saw in class with Professor Barker, to innovate you need to know and understand your client. Often, they can't really explain what they want but thanks to training in innovation, we can understand their desires. Remember what Henry Ford said:

"If I had asked people what they wanted, they would have said faster horses."

The professor tried to explain that it was important to ask but it was more important to identify the hidden desires embedded within the answers.

Thanks to innovation, companies can offer clients fresh experiences, avoiding them becoming bored by the same surprises over and over again. In fact, one way to involve customers is through the co-creation of new experiences.

CO-CREATION:

The professor explained the concept of co-creation, a form of innovation that engaged the most important part of the equation: customers. To illustrate this idea, he quoted a phrase from the renowned professor Philip Kotler:

"Who should design the products or services? The customer, of course."

"Well, this is what co-creation is all about. It's a way for customers to get involved in the creation of new services, products or experiences.

Professor Jones explained that no one better than the user could tell us which parts of the customer experience should be changed, rethought or eliminated. In this way, the client becomes involved in the construction of new solutions that give great experiences to users.

"I'll give you the case of a laboratory that manufactures medicine for children. They realized that their cough medicine, despite being very effective, was not selling as expected."

They invited children with their parents to participate in a co-creation workshop and found that the children didn't like the taste and the dispenser jammed easily. The lab offered a tasting of different flavors and several types of dispensers. Finally, they released a new strawberry flavored medicine with single-dose dispenser that broke sales records. And the children were rewarded with a backpack full of toys.

"You see? With a little creativity and a helping hand from users you can do great things. The new experience of the children in testing the medicine was entirely innovative. You just need an open mind."

"Now, I'm going to give you two examples of customer experience using the Customer Experience Map (MEC) tool."

The teacher sat on the armchair in front of the desk on the elevated platform and began the slide show:

IT´S NOT MAGIC, IT´S CUSTOMER EXPERIENCE STRATEGY

First example: VETERINARY CLINIC

Imagine we are hired as consultants to implement Customer Experience Management in a veterinary clinic. The owner tells us that she rarely gets repeat customers and said she needs to provide an innovative service with remarkable experiences to retain customers and gain their loyalty. We ask which of the animals they treat are the most profitable. The answer is dogs. Thus, our Buyer Persona is a dog owner.

To gather the relevant information, we asked the clinic to provide us with the telephone numbers of clients with dogs to take an in-depth look into their experiences at the clinic.

The following chart summarizes the experience of a specific customer who participated in an interview.

Description of the stages:

1 John needs a nearby veterinary clinic for his sick dog Bobby

2 He goes on-line looking for local clinics and finds the "Veterinary Clinic". The comments are neutral. The website and photos of the clinic seem OK. The site makes some mention of the friendliness of the veterinarian but little else.

3 John decides to give it a try. He has his first bad experience (Pain Point) when he can't find a place to park nearby.

4 When he arrives at the clinic no one receives him or even says hello. It's hot, poorly lit. It smells of animals (sign of poor hygiene). He has to wait for an hour (Pain Point).

5 When he finally sees the veterinarian, she is friendly and charming. She is very gentle and loving with Bobby and examines him without haste. She offers clear and precise explanations (Point of surprise or Wow moment). She schedules an appointment 10 days later, telling John he'll receive an SMS the day before as a reminder.

6 He leaves the clinic and finds he's received a parking ticket (Pain Point).

7 John goes to the pharmacy recommended by the Vet. The experience is fine but nothing more.

8 Nine days later he doesn't receive an SMS, but he has already decided not to go back. John thinks that, although the Vet was friendly, the overall experience was negative.

Summary of in-depth interviews with dog owners

Of all the interviewees:

- 85% report that parking is a serious problem
- 72% think that adhering to the scheduled time is very important
- 77% reported being unhappy with the general condition of the clinic
- 70% said they would appreciate it if someone was there to attend them when they arrived
- 68% believed it was important to receive the SMS because it's easy to forget the appointment

Basic Diagnosis and Opportunities for Improvement:

Overall, the customer experience is very poor, generating negative emotions that will seriously impact both customer loyalty and the reputation of the company.

Firstly, we should focus on finding solutions to the Pain Points. Sometimes this can be as easy as turning up the heat, improving the lighting and cleanliness. It may also be necessary to hire someone, a veterinary assistant, and give them training in emotional intelligence to welcome clients, confirm their data and accompany them to the waiting room. It's also important to optimize the scheduling, using an appointments management app that also automatically sends reminders to clients.

Regarding one of the most important Pain Points, the clinic should consider making an arrangement with a local parking lot to offer free parking for their clients. This could be a Surprise Point or, at least a positive aspect of the experience. If this is not possible, and since this is an important problem for clients, they should consider changing location.

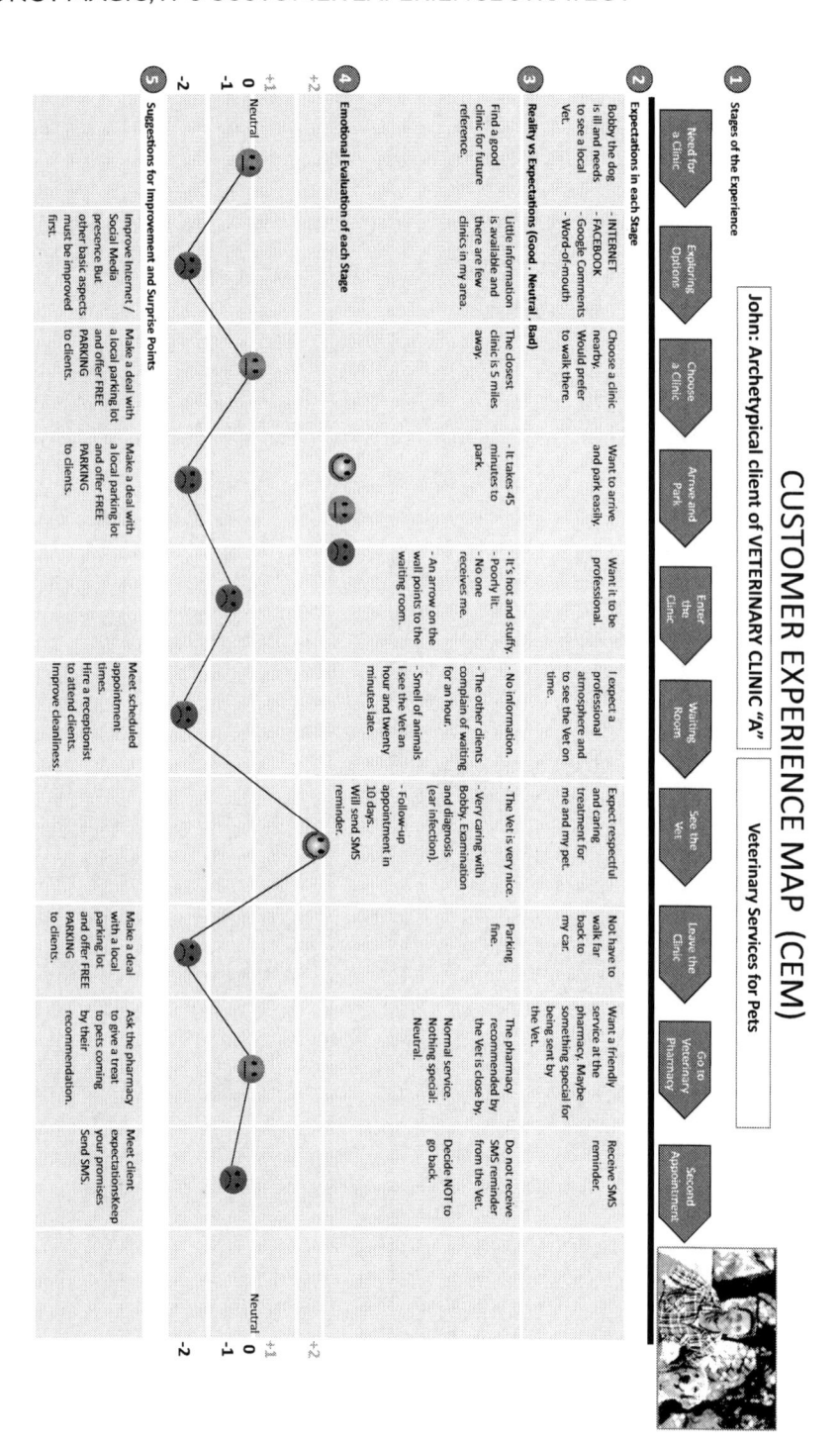

IT´S NOT MAGIC, IT´S CUSTOMER EXPERIENCE STRATEGY

CUSTOMER EXPERIENCE MAP (CEM)

John: Archetypical client of VETERINARY CLINIC "A" — Veterinary Services for Pets

Stages of the Experience

1. Need for a Clinic
2. Exploring Options
3. Choose a Clinic
4. Arrive and Park
5. Enter the Clinic
6. Waiting Room
7. See the Vet
8. Leave the Clinic
9. Go to Veterinary Pharmacy
10. Second Appointment

	1. Need for a Clinic	2. Exploring Options	3. Choose a Clinic	4. Arrive and Park	5. Enter the Clinic	6. Waiting Room	7. See the Vet	8. Leave the Clinic	9. Go to Veterinary Pharmacy	10. Second Appointment
Expectations in each Stage	Bobby the dog is ill and needs to see a local Vet.	- INTERNET - FACEBOOK - Google Comments - Word-of-mouth	Choose a clinic nearby. Would prefer to walk there.	Want to arrive and park easily.	Want it to be professional.	I expect a professional atmosphere and to see the Vet on time.	Expect respectful and caring treatment for me and my pet.	Not have to walk far back to my car.	Want a friendly service at the pharmacy. Maybe something special for being sent by the Vet.	Receive SMS reminder.
Reality vs Expectations (Good . Neutral . Bad)	Find a good clinic for future reference.	Little information is available and there are few clinics in my area.	The closest clinic is 5 miles away.	- It takes 45 minutes to park.	- It´s hot and stuffy. - Poorly lit. - No one receives me. - An arrow on the wall points to the waiting room.	- No information. - The other clients complain of waiting for an hour. - Smell of animals - I see the Vet an hour and twenty minutes late.	- The Vet is very nice. - Very caring with Bobby. Examination and diagnosis (ear infection). - Follow-up appointment in 10 days. Will send SMS reminder.	Parking fine.	The pharmacy recommended by the Vet is close by. Normal service. Nothing special: Neutral.	Do not receive SMS reminder from the Vet. Decide NOT to go back.
Emotional Evaluation of each Stage (+2 / +1 / Neutral / -1 / -2)	Neutral	-1	-1	-2	-1	-2	+2	-1	Neutral	-2
Suggestions for Improvement and Surprise Points	Improve Internet / Social Media presence. But other basic aspects must be improved first.	Make a deal with a local parking lot and offer FREE PARKING to clients.	Make a deal with a local parking lot and offer FREE PARKING to clients.	Meet scheduled appointment times. Hire a receptionist to attend clients. Improve cleanliness.	Make a deal with a local parking lot and offer FREE PARKING to clients.	Ask the pharmacy to give a treat to pets coming by their recommendation.	Meet client expectations. Keep your promises. Send SMS.

Second example:
NUT-PSY-SPO CENTER: Triple Effect

Let's analyze this company that is very focused on putting the client at the center and optimizing the customer experience.

They have innovated in their business model. Almost 100% of their patients are people who had followed traditional diets but regained weight in the medium term. In-depth interviews with patients revealed the following (PAIN POINTS):

Summary of in-depth interviews with patients of other weight-loss clinics

Of all the interviewees:

- 90% reported regaining the weight they lost after they completed the diet because they lacked the proper habits
- 84% said that anxiety was the main cause of regaining weight
- 87% found it hard to keep their weight in check because they didn't have healthy habits or an active lifestyle

Based on the results of the research and using the Customer Experience Map (CEM), they designed a customer experience to help their clients definitively change their lifestyle habits.

They combined nutritional consulting, psychological support and a personal trainer to offer a very successful service. Clients received a friendly and professional service. They also received daily support thanks to an app where they could enter their daily meals as well as their moods and emotional state. In this way, the clinic helped their clients to be aware of their behavior.

CARLOS CORREA RODRÍGUEZ

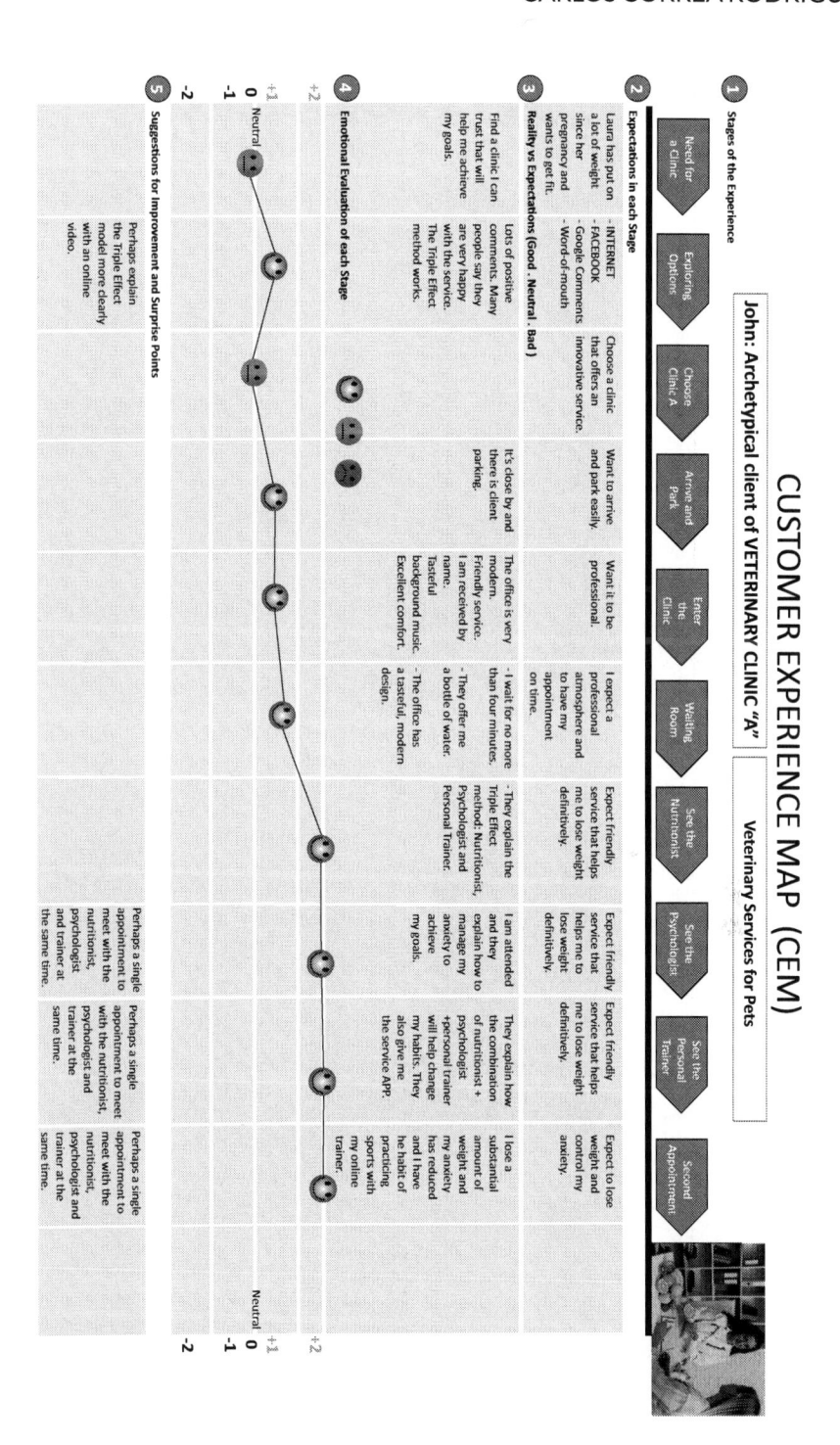

CUSTOMER EXPERIENCE MAP (CEM)

John: Archetypical client of VETERINARY CLINIC "A" | **Veterinary Services for Pets**

1. Stages of the Experience

Need for a Clinic → Exploring Options → Choose Clinic A → Arrive and Park → Enter the Clinic → Waiting Room → See the Nutritionist → See the Psychologist → See the Personal Trainer → Second Appointment

2. Expectations in each Stage

- **Need for a Clinic:** Laura has put on a lot of weight since her pregnancy and wants to get fit.
- **Exploring Options:**
  - INTERNET
  - FACEBOOK
  - Google Comments
  - Word-of-mouth
- **Choose Clinic A:** Choose a clinic that offers an innovative service.
- **Arrive and Park:** Want to arrive and park easily.
- **Enter the Clinic:** Want it to be professional.
- **Waiting Room:** I expect a professional atmosphere and to have my appointment on time.
- **See the Nutritionist:** Expect friendly service that helps me to lose weight definitively.
- **See the Psychologist:** Expect friendly service that helps me to lose weight definitively.
- **See the Personal Trainer:** Expect friendly service that helps me to lose weight definitively.
- **Second Appointment:** Expect to lose weight and control my anxiety.

3. Reality vs Expectations (Good, Neutral, Bad)

- **Need for a Clinic:** Find a clinic I can trust that will help me achieve my goals.
- **Exploring Options:** Lots of positive comments. Many people say they are very happy with the service. The Triple Effect method works.
- **Choose Clinic A:** —
- **Arrive and Park:** It's close by and there is client parking.
- **Enter the Clinic:** The office is very modern. Friendly service. I am received by name. They offer me a bottle of water. Tasteful background music. Excellent comfort.
- **Waiting Room:** I wait for no more than four minutes. - The office has a tasteful, modern design.
- **See the Nutritionist:** They explain the Triple Effect method: Nutritionist, Psychologist and Personal Trainer.
- **See the Psychologist:** I am attended and they explain how to manage my anxiety to achieve my goals.
- **See the Personal Trainer:** They explain how the combination of nutritionist + psychologist + personal trainer will help change my habits. They also give me the service APP.
- **Second Appointment:** I lose a substantial amount of weight and my anxiety has reduced and I have the habit of practicing sports with my online trainer.

4. Emotional Evaluation of each Stage

+2
+1
0 Neutral
-1
-2

5. Suggestions for Improvement and Surprise Points

- **Exploring Options:** Perhaps explain the Triple Effect model more clearly with an online video.
- **See the Nutritionist:** Perhaps a single appointment to meet with the nutritionist, psychologist and trainer at the same time.
- **See the Psychologist:** Perhaps a single appointment to meet with the nutritionist, psychologist and trainer at the same time.
- **See the Personal Trainer:** Perhaps a single appointment to meet with the nutritionist, psychologist and trainer at the same time.

Description of the stages:

1. Laura is looking for a nutritionist because she's put on a lot of weight since giving birth

2. She goes online looking for nearby clinics and finds "NUT-PSY-SPO CENTER: Triple Effect" The comments are very positive. The website is very attractive and intuitive with a chat feature to ask questions and an option to book an appointment immediately. The site also tells her there is free parking for clients. Laura is relieved there will be no hassle about parking and so she decides on that clinic.

3. Laura goes to the clinic, parks easily and takes an elevator to the center.

4. When Laura arrives a very friendly woman greets her, calling her by her name. She notes the tasteful, modern furnishings and comfortable temperature. There is music in the background.

5. A few minutes later she was called by the nutritionist. She explained the methodology of the clinic to help their patients be more healthy and happy. Laura was very pleased (SURPRISE POINT or WOW Moment).

6. Laura then went to the next office to talk with the psychologist who explained how they would help her manage her anxiety. They explained a number of exercises and demonstrated an app to use if Laura had any doubts (SURPRISE POINT or WOW moment).

7. Finally, Laura saw a personal trainer who explained the physical exercise program. He showed Laura the website that showed her daily exercise routine for every week and explained he would monitor her daily progress. Laura was amazed. (SURPRISE POINT or WOW moment).

8. Second appointment: Laura has lost quite a bit of weight and she feels much less anxious and she has followed the instructions of her personal trainer. She is very happy with the daily monitoring. She feels she is changing her daily habits and feeling much better and happier.

9. Laura sings the praises of the clinic to her friends and family. She shares her experience on social media. The clinic has given Laura an incredible customer experience. Although the service is more expensive than a traditional clinic, the Buyer Persona or typical user of the service is willing to pay more for an excellent experience.

After explaining the different uses of the Customer Experience Map, Professor Jones rose from his chair, slotted it away inside the desk, and walked to the center of the classroom. He put his hands together as he spoke to the students:

"I hope you have seen the many benefits the Customer Experience Map tool has to offer. The Map is one of the most important resources of this management system. It will give you extraordinary visibility that you must take advantage of to dazzle your customers. The idea is for them to be thrilled with the experience and can't wait to tell others about it!"

IT´S NOT MAGIC, IT´S CUSTOMER EXPERIENCE STRATEGY

From: Carmen@greenmail.com

To: Marcos@greenmail.com

Subject: DESIGNING EXPERIENCES FOR YOUR BUYER PERSONA

Hi Honey:

Today the professor showed us a very cool and useful tool that can boost the visibility of the relationship customers have with the company. You'll love it. It's called the Customer Experience Map. Basically, it analyzes each of the points of contact the client has with the company in a chronological and orderly way.

For example, if your customers from Monday to Friday are executives who work in offices near the restaurant, you must analyze each stage the client goes through, from how he heard about the restaurant (internet, social media, recommendation of friends, etc.), if he comes by car and has problems parking, if he calls to book ahead, when they get there who greets them, how they are shown to the table, the service by the staff, etc.

It's important to know what the client expects at each stage. That is, maybe they're in a hurry and so want excellent service but quickly and not have to wait long for the dishes or the bill. Find out what the points of contact are and how the client feels at each point. From there you can make improvements, innovate and surprise the client at some points of contact. It's essential that the client perceives that what the restaurant offers has value, otherwise we're just throwing money away.

Remember when we went to the circus with the kids? Getting the tickets by internet was super easy. We automatically received a WhatsApp message with a very funny video of a clown thanking us for buying the tickets. When we arrived, there were circus employees speeding up parking and they directed us to the entrance. There were ushers so we were seated quickly. The show was great and at intermission they were ready with soft drinks, hot dogs and circus merchandise like cups, keys chains, t-shirts, etc. We returned for the second part and everyone loved it. When it was over it was really easy to leave. In fact, there were employees there to direct traffic out of the parking lot and so there were no line ups. It was an amazing customer experience that really stuck in my memory. We even talked about it with our friends and many of them went because of our recommendation. Well that was a successful customer experience.

In class they explained about Pain Points, moments when the client experiences negative emotions such as anger or frustration. There are also the Surprise Points or Wow moments, when clients are amazed by something unexpected. It is important to identify Pain Points, correct them and even turn them into Surprise Points.

Marcos, analyze each stage of the customer experience in the restaurant and we'll talk about it when I get back. I'm attaching two very interesting examples from our class about a veterinary clinic and a weight-loss clinic.

And please make sure Alvaro is prepared for his math exam on Friday!

I love you,

Carmen

IT´S NOT MAGIC, IT´S CUSTOMER EXPERIENCE STRATEGY

CHAPTER 8:
THE SENSES AND EXPERIENCE

Today, a spring storm had broken at dawn that had drenched the campus. Although damp, there was a fresh, invigorating air that was deeply inspiring.

In the classroom Professor Miller was waiting. She was a woman of about 45 years of age, dressed in a light grey and pink Prince of Wales cotton suit. She had sky blue eyes and wore an enigmatic smile. She introduced herself to the students and explained that the class would be about the marketing of the senses or sensory marketing.

She began with a phrase from the philosopher Ramón Llull:

"Each of the five senses is a philosopher"

The professor explained that the philosopher wanted to convey the importance of the senses as a whole and, at the same time, the autonomy of each. She went on to say that, if we applied this idea to the business world, we could conclude that all the senses are involved in producing emotions and in the creation of experiences.

The teacher took off her glasses and continued speaking, holding them in her right hand.

As each sense was autonomous, all five had to be aligned to achieve unforgettable experiences. It made no sense for touch to contradict the eye, for example.

Professor Miller gave an example of a boutique clothing store where a customer was visually struck by a piece of clothing. But when she felt the fabric with her hand, she realized she didn't like the feel.

"Touch spoke badly to the eye about the garment and the sale was lost. The idea is that the senses "speak well" to the others about their perceptions," she said, making quotation marks with her fingers.

She pointed out that this example could be extrapolated to any other sector. She offered the case of the baking industry where boutique bakeries have proliferated. Here, customers are attracted primarily by the smell of freshly baked bread. It is then essential that the taste and the texture of the bread match the smell.

"Remember that experiences are holistic. That's why all the senses must be combined and linked to each other. Otherwise, the experience will suffer through the sense, or senses, where the appeal is weakest".

Professor Miller continued with her explanation on how to make use of the senses to create experiences. She mentioned there are essentially two channels: the physical or traditional and the digital, emphasizing that both were equally important. According to the latest trends, and depending on the sector, customers interacted through both channels when making their purchasing decisions. Thus, it was essential to create an excellent multi-channel sensory experience.

"A great number of people, before going to a physical establishment, visit the website, browse the products online, look at comments on Facebook, Instagram, etc. From this they decide whether to go or not. This is true of a law firm, a transport company, a pharmacy, a clinic or a fast-food restaurant.

She went on to explain that companies must strive to provide an excellent sensory experience, regardless of the channel. All five senses must be engaged to create sensory experiences that are pleasant, fun, simple and enjoyable. The goal is for the client to buy again and again, and so create a connection and loyalty to the brand.

"OK. Now we are going to study a crucial aspect of this topic. How to increase company revenue through the efficient management of the different senses in both channels. We will see how each of them impacts our purchasing decisions, both individually and in combination with the others and how they are the source of experience."

Professor Miller projected the following image onto the screen:

SIGHT:

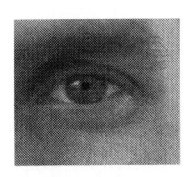

This sense is the most persuasive. The aim is to engrave an image in the mind of the client. Between 80% and 90% of the information perceived by our brain is visual. For more than 85% of customers color is a very important factor in their purchasing decisions. Color is what differentiates brands and logos for most consumers. Furniture, designs, the warmth of colors, signage, etc. all are important in persuading customers in their purchasing. Everything from a dessert to a watch to a handbag enters through the eyes. Visual marketing is about keeping the object in your subconscious until one day you decide to buy it.

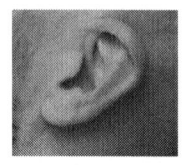

HEARING:

Music is a very powerful marketing tool. It helps associate a brand with modernism, dynamism or freshness depending on the music. Current popular music is used in clothing stores for younger customers. It also helps us associate a brand with the concept of elegance. For example, in an elegant restaurant with a customer profile of people between 45 and 65 years of age they may have subtle, classical music playing in the background.

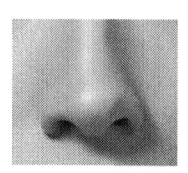

SMELL:

Essences and fragrances can stimulate the purchase of certain products. Smells can transmit feelings of comfort, peace, freshness, etc. Like colors, smells produce a mental image of a brand. I may like it, dislike it or feel indifferent. However, too much of a smell can be unpleasant. For example, enter a clothing store and that characteristic smell of new clothes is very strong, even outside the shop.

Another classic example of olfactory marketing is the smell of popcorn when entering the cinema. We closely associate cinema with the smell of popcorn, even though we may not consciously perceive the smell. Similarly, when we open a pack of chips there is a powerful smell of the flavorings, stimulating our salivary glands to make us want to eat them.

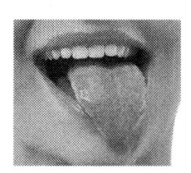

TASTE:

Taste works in combination with other senses, particularly smell and sight. When we taste a certain brand of coffee or type of wine, at the same time we are smelling it and seeing its color. And it is this combination of the senses that determines if we buy it or not.

It may happen that we buy a cake for its color and texture and even smell. But if, at the moment of truth, it doesn't taste as expected we feel deeply disappointed. All the senses must be aligned so that the experience is unforgettable. Companies that sell snacks usually add flavors to enhance the taste, activating a reward system in the brain so you eat them compulsively without stopping. The famous advertising slogan for a brand of chips is "Bet you can't eat just one!"

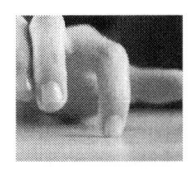

TOUCH:

We touch to feel the surface of materials, textures and weight that we may perceive as synonymous with quality. Touch generates rational and emotional information about the products we touch and about the brands we buy. Touch is a final decision maker. We touch what attracts us visually. One brand of professional cameras realized that, apart from its technical attributes and specifications, clients often weighed different cameras in their hands. The company decided to make their cameras a little heavier since their clients associated weight with quality.

Music influences mood. The better the mood, the greater the predisposition to buy something. Music also makes us associate certain attributes to a brand, for example, the music used in an advertising spot.

Professor Miller went on to explain that stimulating the senses was the key to generating pleasant experiences. This in turn would spur clients to buy more and even to recommend the experience to others.

"The key to creating experiences is to stimulate the senses"

The professor then introduced a new concept called intensity of experience. This referred to how an experience can activate the customer's senses and associate them to a greater or lesser degree with a specific brand.

"When we get a client to actively participate in the experience, it will have a higher level of intensity than another in which the client is a passive participant".

To illustrate this same idea, the professor showed the students a slide showing the classifications of the specialist in experiential marketing, Dr. Bernd H. Schmitt. He categorized experiences based on their capacity to generate more or less connection with the client.

TYPES OF EXPERIENCES

PRAGMATIC	Sensorial or aesthetic	Feelings or affect	Intellectual or educational	Action	Relational
	1	**2**	**3**	**4**	**5**
Price Selection Quality Promotion Usability Accessibility	Perceive **Make the client perceive** Colors Sounds Smells Forms Design Furnishings Lighting Temperature	Feel **Make the client feel** Images Customer Service Courtesies Videos Smells Lighting	Think **Make the client think** Graphic information Production/Function Videos Personal	Interact **Make the client touch and interact** Product samples Experimentation Tastings Courses	Relate **Make the client integrate** Clubs Communities Activities Courses Entertainment

Adaptation of the model by Schmitt, B.H. (2003 & 2010) with contributions from Dubé, L. & Lebel, J.L. (2003); Gentile, C., Spiller, N. & Noci, G. (2007) and Brakus, J.J. (2009).

0. Pragmatic experiences:

Those in which customers can acquire a product without involving feelings and emotions. In these cases, the user looks for aspects such as utility, price, sales, technical quality or availability of the product. For example, buying a hammer in a hardware store or a table in an outlet where they give you the chairs for free and you immediately take them home in your car.

1. Sensorial or aesthetic experiences:

Here the client, although passive, perceives colors, music, fragrances, lighting, aesthetics, etc. These could be experiences when entering a dental clinic with designer furniture, warm lighting, the right temperature, etc.

2. Feelings or affective experiences:

These appeal to the mood of the customer, to the emotions generated at the moment of consumption. You want to make the user comfortable, cheerful and motivated to buy. For example, in a clothing store where the service from employees, the music, lighting or smells produce positive feelings about purchasing.

3. Intellectual or educational experiences:

These aim to involve the consumer's intellect and creativity to solve a problem in relation to the products or services that the company offers. For example, when a bank offers you a pension plan, you use your intellect to decide on whether it is a good option for your future financial security. Alternatively, if in a restaurant you see photographs of famous artists with the chef, you think the restaurant is good since we associate celebrities with quality.

4. Action experiences:

Here the client is no longer a passive subject but is actively engaged. The goal is to create experiences related to the senses, lifestyles, interaction with others, etc. For example, a gourmet shop wants to rank the best wines in its wine cellar and invites representative customers and a gastronomic influencer to a wine tasting. After the tasting, they post news of the event and the experience and comments of the participants on their website and on social media, including their recommendations. Customers are encouraged to talk about the wines with others with a similar consumer profile, offering them attractive special discounts.

5. Relational experiences:

These are when clients enjoy social and cultural experiences, while connecting with other people with the same interests. Here the user plays an active role, relating to the brand and to their peers. For example, a hairdresser or chain of hairdressers invite their clients to a fashion show with hairstyles done by the company and clients vote for the winners. Here customers interact with the brand and with other participants. The company will make product recommendations and offer discounts for future haircuts, treatments, etc.

"Well, class, what do you think about this classification of experiences? Do you find them useful to apply to your companies? Don't forget that the experiences that most engage with the brand are those of action and relationship."

"The experiences that most attract our clients to the brand are those that actively engage them.
These are experiences of action and relation"

"To illustrate Schmitt's adapted classification, I am going to give you an example that goes through all the experiential phases. As you will see, these are ordered from less to more engagement."

IT´S NOT MAGIC, IT´S CUSTOMER EXPERIENCE STRATEGY

THE ROYAL SCHOOL OF CONFECTIONERY

It is a fictitious company that sells cakes and fine pastries for special events, restaurants, cafes, etc. They have several bakeries/shops around the country. It also has another line of business selling ingredients such as special flours, sugars exclusive, low-calorie sweeteners, gourmet chocolates and cocoa, homemade jams, seasonal sugared fruits, as well as baking molds, pastry bags, trays and other culinary equipment.

1 Sensorial or aesthetic experience / Passive / 1 Perception / Capture attention:

The entrance of the shop has a display of chocolate and gold colors, giving a feeling of elegance, refinement and prestige. There's a large window so you can see the kitchen and the confectioners working in their uniforms. The light and temperature are perfect for the time of year.

2 Feelings or affective experiences / Passive / Feeling / Create feeling:

Confectioners are painstakingly at work, using tongs to perfectly decorate the cakes and pastries. In the shop there is a pleasingly subtle aroma of chocolate, fruits and jams. The staff are smiling, friendly and very helpful.

3 Intellectual or educational experiences / Passive / Thinking / Provoke thought:

The pastry and cake boxes have a very elegant design, with a note indicating the origin of the ingredients and the name of the pastry chef. On their website and on social media they offer interesting tips on new trends in confectionery, ecological ingredients, etc. They interview their bakers and post the videos on social media. They want the client to want to pay more for a high quality, exclusive product.

4 Action experiences / Active / Interacting / Touching and participating:

Twice a year they invite their most regular and profitable customers to taste new cakes and pastries. They ask for suggestions for new creations and so adapt their products to the tastes and desires of their customers.

If a customer makes an innovative suggestion that helps them co-create an interesting product, they mention of the customer's name in marketing the product.

5 Relational experiences / Active / Interacting / Becoming part of a community:

They hold three baking workshops a year, explaining the tricks and techniques of great confectioners. This encourages clients to interact with each other. Once a year they have baking contests for clients of the business line selling bakery supplies and equipment. The contestants send photos of their work using an app developed by the company, where they can interact with other contestants and exchange tips and tricks of the trade. After the visual presentation, there is a taste-test by experts and prizes are awarded. This provides entertainment and builds a community and relationships among the clients.

"I hope that this example clarifies the different levels of experience depending on the relationship with the client."

Professor Miller commented that Schmitt's adapted model was applicable, with possible modifications, to any industry and sector.

She added that at all levels of experience there was a very important factor which must never be overlooked: the employee.

"You will study this with Professor Brown tomorrow. You'll love it," she concluded with a broad smile.

From: Carmen@greenmail.com

To: Marcos@greenmail.com

Subject: FEELINGS AND EXPERIENCES

Good morning, Honey:

I hope you are getting along OK with the house, the kids and the restaurant. I'll be back soon!

Today we were with Professor Miller talking about how to generate experiences. She told us there are experiences where the client has a passive role and others where they have an active role and even relate to each other. The latter are the ones that build the most customer loyalty by making them feel part of the company.

For example, in the restaurant there are affective, sensory experiences with colors, aesthetics, smells, temperature, the service from the waiters, the chef and even you as manager. Educational experiences can also be created by giving nutritional information about the dishes, for example, if they are high in protein, low in fat, locally sourced, lactose-free, asparagus from Navarre, Rioja wine, etc. Here the customer has a passive role, but they are equally important.

On the other hand, there are experiences of action and relationship, which are the ones that most build customer loyalty. Remember my email about segmentation, the Empathy Map and the Buyer Persona? Well, imagine we find out that our customers play padel and that many are also businesspeople. It may be a good idea to organize a paddle tournament and then hold a lunch in the restaurant. That way we can create relationships between them. And since they are businesspeople, we can give them an opportunity to present themselves and build contacts. If they do establish business relationships because of us, imagine how loyal they will be to the restaurant. Look, I just had a creative inspiration! You can call it the "PLB Event" (Paddle, Lunch and Business) What do you think? 😌

    I love you, Carmen

CHAPTER 9:
PEOPLE WHO LOOK AFTER PEOPLE

Today was a special day at business school. As every year, Professor Brown returned to give her Masterclass on employees or 'internal customers' as she called them. She was a much-loved teacher. Before dedicating herself to consulting, she worked in the human resources department of the school for 10 years. She was responsible for many innovations that had fundamentally changed the concept of the staff within the school and of the school among the staff.

She was now working as an external advisor to the business school's personnel department.

Professor Brown was about 46 years of age, elegant, with green eyes and a youthful style. Since entering the classroom, she wore a sincere smile on her face highlighted by her lipstick and pale complexion. The teacher approached each student, read the sign indicating their names and asked each how they felt. Many answered with a smile "Good".

"I'm Professor Brown. I'm very happy to be back at the school and reunited with old friends, teachers and staff. Great people who make beautiful things happen between these walls."

Most of the students noted and commented on the friendliness of the school staff. During coffee breaks and lunch the teachers sat with the students and chatted about the business world but also their families and other apparently more trivial issues. Did the warm atmosphere at the school have something to do with Professor Brown?

"I work as a personnel consultant for different companies all over the country. I also give lectures on talent and human capital, among other things."

The professor continued talking about the idea of a people-focused company. She proposed a general concept summed up in one sentence: "a company is a place, both physical and digital, where people take care of people."

The professor wrote this sentence on the board. She noted that almost all of the students were writing down the phrase in their notebooks.

"You can't undertake a customer experience management project without taking into account the experience of the people who work in the company. It doesn't matter if it's a company of 5, 50 or 5,000 employees. These are the people who offer the services or final products to the client. That's why taking care of them is so important if you want them to go the extra mile in offering a unique customer experience."

She went on to say that, in her experience as a constant, she had seen how some companies insisted on offering their customers a better experience, but without taking into account their employees. "To be successful externally we must be successful internally." At this point, the professor paused for emphasis before providing the students with a striking statistic:

"According to a number of studies, 80% of customers who abandon a company do so because of poor customer experience in employee and customer interaction"

"Don't you think this detail makes it important to pay attention to employees?" the teacher asked.

EMOTIONS OF THE EMPLOYEES

Professor Brown pointed out that managing the emotions of employees or internal customers was essential to offering excellent customer experiences and, as research has shown, increase company profitability.

The professor quoted Mahatma Gandhi, who claimed that life was like a mirror:

"Life has taught me that people are kind, if I am kind; that people are sad, if I am sad; that everyone loves me, if I love them; that they are all bad, if I hate them; that there are smiling faces, if I smile at them; that there are bitter faces, if I am bitter; that the world is happy, if I am happy."

"By the way, class, does anyone know what mirror neurons are?" I'll tell you:

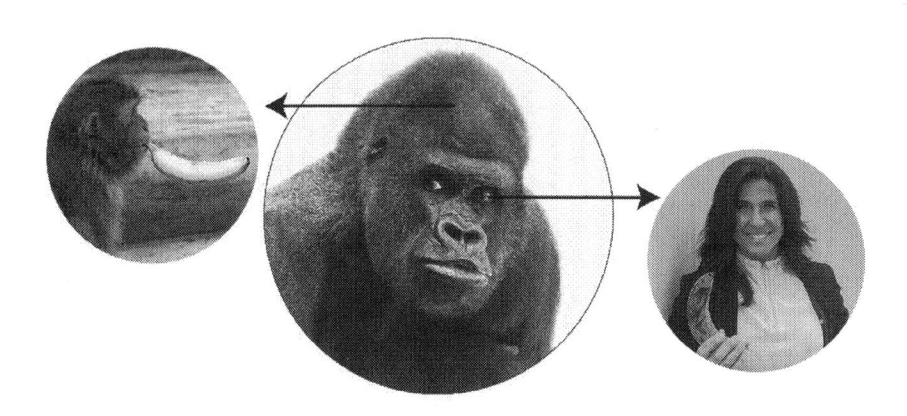

Professor Brown explained to the class how the Russian neurologist Giacomo Rizzolatti discovered in his research with monkeys that they imitated the movements of humans. He realized that when monkeys imitated humans, a neural network was activated which he called 'mirror neurons'.

"I mention this not because some of you remind me of monkeys." The class laughed at the comment.

Research shows that we not only imitate mechanical behavior, such as picking up a pencil, but also emulate emotions. In other words, we are affected by the emotions of those around us. If a friend is sad, we become sad. If we read a funny book, we are happy. These neurons regulate, among other things, empathy. They are also part of learning by observation.

> «Emotions are contagious thanks to mirror neurons. Knowing this is essential in managing the emotions of employees. I can't have happy customers without happy employees."

Professor Brown described employees as the bridge between the company and the customer. Company management must never overlook this strategic and essential aspect as any customer experience management project.

The professor paused a moment to sip some water, and continued:

"Starting from the premise that employees are internal customers, we are going to establish a parallel with what Professor Jones taught you about customer experience management. Let's start with a similar tool but this time focused on the employee. This is called the Employee Experience Map

THE EMPLOYEE EXPERIENCE MAP (EEM)

Professor Brown explained that the Employee Experience Map (EEM) dealt with the different stages of the employee experience from first joining the company until their departure.

The teacher projected a slide on the screen next to the board.

1 Inquire: Potential candidates look for information on the Internet and ask around about the company. It is important that the company has a good reputation so that it attracts the talent it needs.

2 Selection Process: We must be clear about the profile the company is looking for, the department where they will work and the tasks they will perform, and consequently, what knowledge and skills the candidate must have. This refers to their academic knowledge and skills such as problem-solving, teamworking, friendliness, kindness, humility, motivation in learning, availability, flexibility, etc.

"Attention class! In a company that focuses on generating unique experiences for its customers it is essential to 'select people who like people'. A Master's degree in data management is worthless if you don't like to work with others" said the professor, raising her index finger to call their attention.

"I always recommend asking for references from the 3 top candidates for the position. It is crucial to learn from the experiences of others and so minimize the risk of making a mistake in the selection."

3 Hiring: The person who passes all the filters now joins the company. We must now make the incorporation process as pleasant as possible. We present the new recruit to their colleagues; we tell them as much as possible about the company; we explain our strategy of generating positive customer experiences, our vision of customer service, and so on. It is highly recommended that part of their salary be linked to customer feedback on the experience they provide.

4 The daily routine: In this phase, the employee is fully integrated and must be given opportunities for growth and training; performance must be evaluated in line with the philosophy of the company, such as, the improvement of services, innovation in experiences, contribution of creative ideas to differentiate the company, etc.

5 Consolidate: Good employees should be offered a career plan, although this can be more difficult in small or medium-sized companies. Here increases in salary can be considered depending on the value, commitment and contribution to the company. In a company with a customer-centered philosophy, bonusses and variable remuneration must be focused on achieving better customer experiences. Complications may arise such as illness, conflicts, etc. which must be resolved or overcome.

6 Change and exit: Professional relationships have a beginning and an end, either due to retirement or new opportunities or changes. Therefore, this phase must be very well planned and must be negotiated with generosity, allowing for pleasant farewells to colleagues, customers, etc. Whenever possible we want to leave a good taste in the mouth of the employee and for them to remember us with affection.

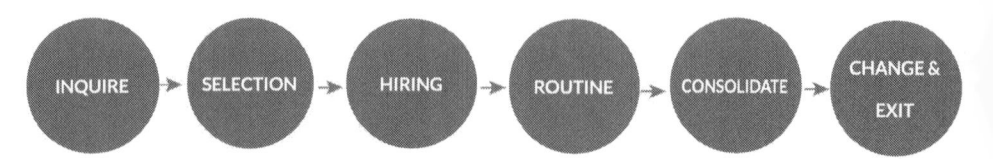

INQUIRE → SELECTION → HIRING → ROUTINE → CONSOLIDATE → CHANGE & EXIT

"For this employee experience map to be effective, we must get to know them. Not all employees are the same or have the same goals or priorities in life. As you saw with Professor Barker, I will show you some basic guidelines to get to know your employees thoroughly.

GUIDELINES TO KNOW THE EMPLOYEE BETTER AND CREATE SPECIAL EXPERIENCES FOR EMPLOYEES:

1 Segmentation: Not all employees are the same or have the same interests or concerns. Knowing where they live, their priorities, their environment, if they have children, if they've just got a divorce, etc., will allow us to have some flexibility when determining their responsibilities and schedules, and to support them in difficult moments.

2 Empathy Map: This is about knowing the employee on a more emotional plane. Knowing what they like, dislike, their challenges, joys and aspirations in the company. Here we can find out if they want to move up and may be an ideal candidate for positions of more responsibility, or if, for example, they've just bought a house and are anxious about meeting their mortgage payments. In the latter case, we can transmit peace of mind in relation to their work and future in the company.

3 Employee persona: If the company has a lot of employees, after conducting segmentation and creating Empathy Maps, employees with similar rational and emotional profiles and work to make them feel more engaged with the company. We can identify various employee archetypes and, based on these, offer certain individuals responsibilities in leading a project, to open a new office, to take charge of a service or innovation or simply do a basic task in an excellent way. Not all employees should be leaders. Basic tasks are also important.

In short, we need to involve employees in the business project. For this, it is necessary they feel heard, that their ideas matter and their merits recognized in public. This will keep them emotionally positive and their creativity will skyrocket. We must in some way reward their contribution of ideas to improve customer experience, to reduce costs or to eliminate processes that do not add value, etc.

PHASES TO MAKE WORK EASIER FOR EMPLOYEES AND STANDARDIZE THE CUSTOMER EXPERIENCE

Professor Brown continued by explaining that once we had designed the employee experience map and identified the rational and emotional aspects with our segmentation tools, Empathy Map and Employee Persona, we had to explain "the rules of the game" to employees.

"Many companies, especially small and medium-sized ones, don't provide clear rules or instructions and, logically, new employees can feel lost. This means that people make mistakes, give poor or inappropriate service to customers and, consequently, lose sales. At the same time, employees can feel stressed by not knowing what to do in a given situation."

The professor turned to the board and wrote: "Design Technical Instructions". She insisted that it was essential to standardize the service; that all employees must deal with customers equally well, so the final experience did not depend on whether you were served by Juan, Marta or Pedro.

To this Professor Brown added that these instructions were living documents, to be rewritten and updated based on feedback from customers and employees.

"A fundamental aspect the instructions should deal with, in the greatest detail possible, are the Surprise Points or Wow Moments. Each employee must have the proper skills and training to deliver them successfully," Brown said walking across the classroom.

The teacher approached the blackboard, rolled up her right sleeve and wrote: "Education and Training'. She explained that not only must instructions be written down, but they should be the basis of employee training. This will help ensure that the level of service perceived by customers will be as consistently good as possible and, therefore, their experience with our company.

"I remember a very nice consulting project I worked with. It was a chain of auto repair shops. The owners noticed that at some shops customers were more loyal, brought their cars in regularly and even recommended their services to friends and family. But others had low customer satisfaction, with bad feedback on social media, and so on." The teacher leaned against the table as she continued. "Imagine how that impacted the company's bottom line. So. The first step was to interview the most dissatisfied customers. They told us their experience as clients was very bad, deadlines were not met and communication was poor. Do you know what we did to standardize the customer experience?" she asked, pausing a few seconds to draw the students' attention. "We updated the technical instructions, involved the employees, getting them to contribute ideas on how to improve the service and, finally, we made a step-by-step video at the shop with the best ratings in customer experience. The idea was to replicate the same service in other shops. 'A picture is worth a thousand words'. This way we activate the mirror neurons, remember?" she added with a smile.

Professor Brown went on, telling the students that once we had training on the technical instructions it was time to "Apply". The next step was to ensure that all employees involved in generating experiences were doing so correctly. She insisted that investing time and resources was the key to generating special experiences for our customers. She repeated again that this was an essential aspect of company strategy and the source of its competitive advantage.

"Now it's time to "Ensure". Let me explain; we must have the necessary tools to confirm that all the work we have done is effective. That is, that we're generating delighted customers, willing to share the wonders of our company in their circles. We do this through surveys, through feedback from customers/friends or by using the mystery shopper tool.

After a brief pause, the professor resumed her talk with the last step that she called "Align". This had a lot to do with the remuneration policy. For the employee it should be very clear that part of their salary should be focused on generating exceptional experiences for customers. That's why the company's strategy should be aligned with the skill of generating experiences.

"Just as a salesperson has a variable salary, paid by performance or units sold, companies oriented towards customer experience will offer a variable salary depending on the degree of satisfaction, loyalty and recommendations of customers. The point is not to lose focus," she stressed.

The teacher waited until the students took their notes before clearing the blackboard.

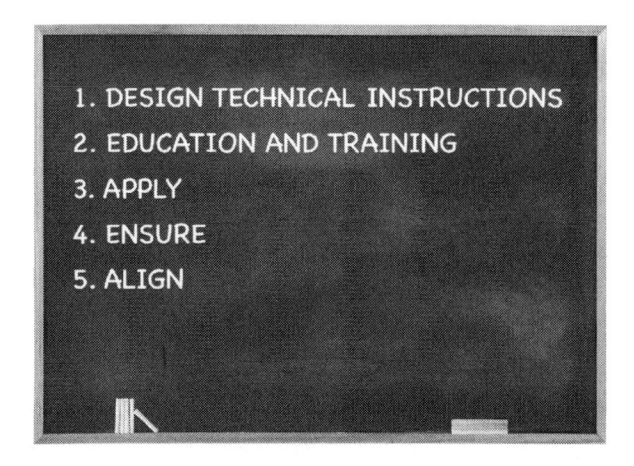

> 1. DESIGN TECHNICAL INSTRUCTIONS
> 2. EDUCATION AND TRAINING
> 3. APPLY
> 4. ENSURE
> 5. ALIGN

Professor Brown concluded this point by stating that the purpose of employee experience management was to have committed, happy workers who were ambassadors for the company to their friends and acquaintances. In short, they felt proud to belong to the company.

PROFILE OF THE CUSTOMER EXPERIENCE EMPLOYEE:

Professor Brown projected a final slide showing the ideal profile of a Customer Experience employee.

1 They like people: They are employees who care about others, like to share and help.

2 Very aware of customers: They may be waiters, lawyers, pharmacists, tax advisors or department store clerks, but they are aware of whether customers need something and if they can facilitate a purchase.

3 They contribute ideas: They collaborate in generating ideas, making it easier to serve the client and simplify logistics. Online purchases are quicker and reduce line-ups during peak hours.

4 Vocation of service: They are convinced their work is important to their clients. They know that this attitude helps make their company more competitive and that their customers feel they are important to the company.

5 Enthusiasts: They have the ability to improve on circumstances, able to turn a customer's complaint into an opportunity to build loyalty and so optimize the customer's experience. They see opportunities in problems, and they love a challenge.

6 Friendly and polite: They are open, empathetic and have a positive attitude in the face of different circumstances. They have a sincere smile that is contagious. At the same time, they are respectful, know how to respect limits and pay attention to details.

7 Creative: They think in an original way and are able to generate new ideas for a new or better customer experience. They are observant and able to identify opportunities for differentiation in Pain Points.

8 Punctual and responsible: They are aware that respecting the rules and schedules of the company is key, committed to fulfilling their obligations.

They like people

Contribute ideas

Enthusiastic

Creative

Client oriented

Vocation of service

Friendly and polite

Punctual and responsible

The professor ended her talk with a phrase from the famous British businessman Richard Branson:

"Clients do not come first. Employees come first. If you take care of your employees, they will take care of the clients."

"With this reflection by Branson, I will conclude the class. This entrepreneur knows what he's talking about. He's founded over 350 companies and always puts the employee experience first as the strategic basis for success of his projects. Will you do the same from now on?"

IT´S NOT MAGIC, IT´S CUSTOMER EXPERIENCE STRATEGY

From: Carmen@greenmail.com

To: Marcos@greenmail.com

Subject: PEOPLE WHO TAKE CARE OF PEOPLE

Hi honey:

I hope everything is fine at home and at the restaurant. Today we had a very interesting class given by a former member of the human resources department of the school. She made us aware of how important it is to have happy employees so they can serve customers well and create excellent experiences. We need employees who are committed to service, who like people and who are attentive and pay attention to details. We should design instructions for dealing with clients, give them training and encourage them with part of their salary to comply with instructions. It is essential to involve employees in making the customer experience special. We also have to segment them, as you already did with customers. To make groups according to their concerns and motivations, both at the rational and emotional level. This way we can help make their experience as employees as pleasant as possible and that will impact the customer experience. As my boss always says: "give to receive".

Do you remember when we were in New York having dinner near Central Park? We were amazed by the welcome they gave us, how friendly and attentive the waiters were, plus the food was great. When we left, they said they "hope to see you again" and they even gave me a rose. Lovely!

Well, I'm sure part of their salary depends on generating that type of customer experience. It's important that the waiters, the maître'd, the chefs, etc. are all customer service oriented. That makes things so much easier when it comes to taking advantage of training.

Well honey, today was a hard day. Think about all this and write down your thoughts.

I'll be back in no time!

I love you,

Carmen

IT´S NOT MAGIC, IT´S CUSTOMER EXPERIENCE STRATEGY

CHAPTER 10:
MEASURE, MEASURE AND MEASURE

Today was a sad day for the students. The course was coming to an end and although it had been very intense, the students had become fond of the teachers and the center. A perceptible air of melancholy hung in the atmosphere. The day would be shorter than usual because after class, they would have a cocktail party with the president of the business school and the rest of the professors.

Professor Brody was waiting in the classroom. She was a young woman, around 35, wearing a black two-button suit with a casual style and modern glasses with lots of personality. In her hands she held a tailor's measuring tape.

"Good morning, customer experience management experts" she said smiling, acknowledging the skills the students had acquired in the program. "I am Professor Brody and today it is time to measure, measure and measure."

Professor Brody began her class with a quote from the famous Professor Peter F Drucker:

"You can't manage what you can't measure"

The professor explained that, when implementing a differentiation strategy based on customer experience, we must have certain control indicators so we know if we're on the right track. These indicators had to measure, among other things, customer/company interactions. These would make it easier for us to know what was working and what was not. We could also identify the most important day-to-day benchmarks so clients enjoyed a better experience. Also, these would help reduce the response times for Pain Points since problems are detected quickly and resolved quickly.

At the same time, measuring also made employees aware of the importance of constantly watching the levels of customer satisfaction and loyalty. It was also useful to better understand customers and so adapt experience to meet their tastes.

"In short, measuring the customer experience helps us never forget how important it is to keep customer desires in mind on a day-to-day basis. It also makes it easier to act quickly if there is a problem and to turn a Pain Point into a Wow moment."

Professor Brody raised the tailor's meter with both hands and saying:

"Just as in the fashion industry they use this meter to measure the client and make clothes to meet their needs and desires, so any company focused on the customer experience needs different tools to evaluate these experiences."

She put the meter aside and went to the blackboard:

1 Customer Satisfaction Score (CSAT): This tells us the level of customer satisfaction in achieving their goals or desires. We find this out through customer surveys.

2 Net Promoter Score (NPS): This is the most important indicator of the customer experience. It is very revealing to know if the client would recommend a company to their friends, acquaintances or others.

3 Loyalty Indicator (LI): This measures the level of satisfaction, recommendation and the intention to buy again.

%DETRACTORS   %NEUTRAL   %PROMOTERS

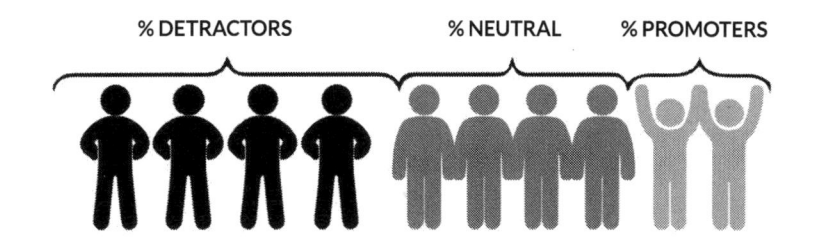

4 Customer Effort Score (CES): This evaluates the degree of difficulty experienced by the client in buying from the company. If it is easy, simple and fun, clients enjoy a better experience than if it is complex and arduous.

5 Complaints Indicator: This is the number of complaints arising from interactions with customers. It is subdivided into complaints that are resolved and unresolved and resolution times.

6 Conversion rate: This tells us if the client will speak well of the company to others.

7 Retention Level or Churn Rate: This measures the time clients remain with the company. This is known as the Churn Rate. This serves to determine the level of customer retention and their average time with the company. It gives a ratio of the number of customers who leave out of the total number of customers.

"This is Forrester's Pyramid," continued the professor, "which is another way to measure the customer experience. As customers, we want our needs to be satisfied quickly and easily. Immediacy is becoming a critical aspect of the customer experience. We don't want to wait in line or wait to be attended. We also want the purchasing process to be very easy, and not have to have a degree in computer science to buy online. The easier the experience, the better. Finally, the experience must be positive, must be fun and give us pleasure.

IT´S NOT MAGIC, IT´S CUSTOMER EXPERIENCE STRATEGY

To know the customer experience we can ask these questions:

1. Did the company meet their needs efficiently?
2. Is it easy to buy from the company, in person or online, or to do business with the company?
3. Did they enjoy buying or doing business with the company?

Professor Brody concluded that the strategy of customer experience management should include, from the very beginning, a basic

CLIENT EXPERIENCE PYRAMID AND EXPERIENCE INDICATORS

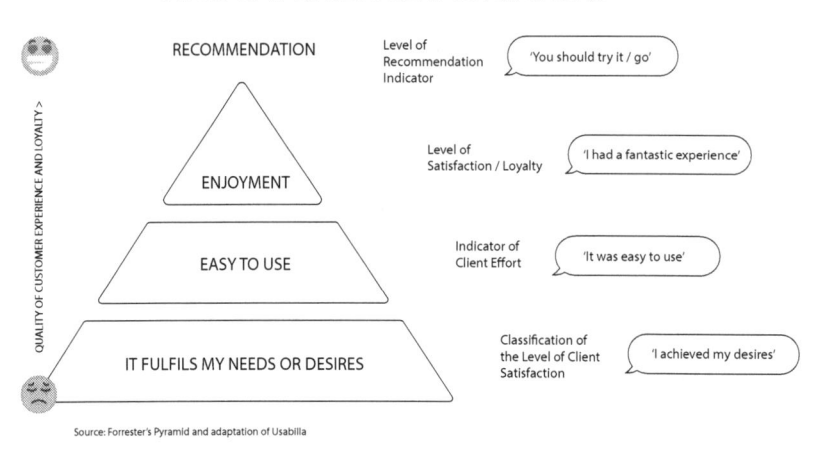

Pyramid Level	Indicator	Customer Quote
RECOMMENDATION	Level of Recommendation Indicator	'You should try it / go'
ENJOYMENT	Level of Satisfaction / Loyalty	'I had a fantastic experience'
EASY TO USE	Indicator of Client Effort	'It was easy to use'
IT FULFILS MY NEEDS OR DESIRES	Classification of the Level of Client Satisfaction	'I achieved my desires'

Source: Forrester's Pyramid and adaptation of Usabilla

series of indicators that evolve over time. It was pointless to start with great desire measuring everything and then not have tools to do so. She recommended starting with the most basic indicators and gradually incorporating more. Furthermore, indicators of the customer experience should also be linked with economic or financial indicators.

"CEM indicators must be aligned with the company's management indicators such as sales, profit margins, salaries, etc. Employee salaries can be linked, for example, to the level of customer experience. The better the customer experience, the lower the churn rate and number of complaints, while the level of recommendation will be higher."

She went on to explain that, on a regular basis, the indicators should be analyzed to correct and refine the level of experience offered to customers. Within the company, it was important to give employees visibility, especially those with direct contact with the client, making them feel involved in successes and also responsible for finding innovative solutions to failures.

"Well class, it has been a pleasure to share this time with you. Now let's go to the Magnum Room, where we will get together with all the professors from the course. And the president will say a few words of thanks".

IT´S NOT MAGIC, IT´S CUSTOMER EXPERIENCE STRATEGY

CHAPTER 11: ONE YEAR LATER

Today we are celebrating the first anniversary of the new restaurant of Marcos and Carmen called "Marcos Gourmet Experiences". This new version looks much more like what they dreamed of when they first saw the 'FOR SALE' sign.

After a year of hard work, they managed to achieve a major transformation, going from being 'just another restaurant' to a meeting place for top executives and managers of important companies in Madrid.

By making a client segmentation, they identified the profile of the most profitable and recurring customer. These were executives and managers from companies in the city. When multinational companies received colleagues from other countries, the restaurant was an ideal place to eat and make a good impression.

By making Empathy Maps, they found that the target customers were interested in healthy eating, wines, training and sports, such as padel, tennis, golf and running, in addition to business matters. They were also looking for an exclusive environment with a touch of glamor but down to earth at the same time.

From Monday to Thursday, target clients wanted to have their meals fairly quickly as they had little time, while on Fridays they were more relaxed and could take their time.

Thanks to what he'd learned, Marcos realized that emotions were the key to developing his business. And so he and Carmen designed a set of memorable sensory experiences for customers.

At the start, by applying the customer experience map, they detected that the most repeated Pain Points were: poor service from the waiters, slowness of the service, difficulty parking, limited privacy to talk about business, the small font on the menu and the lack of dynamism on the menu. In short, the restaurant offered "more of the same" and so did not give the client any reason to repeat the experience much less to recommend it.

They set to work to eliminate these Pain Points or even turn them into Surprise Points or Wow moments. To do this, they made the following changes:

They gave the staff training in Customer Experience Management, changing the concept of a waiter to that of a provider of gastronomic experiences. They established instructions and protocols for dealing with the client, where the first step was to receive the client by name with a sincere smile. Marcos designed a variable salary structure depending on the quality of experience perceived by the client. The task was not easy. Some of the staff were resistant to change, but Marcos had a clear idea of the profile of experience provider he wanted for the restaurant. A consulting company in human resources defined the employee profile he wanted. To improve the speed of the orders they introduced new technology and also made daily posts on social media, the website and the restaurant app, suggestions of dishes and new menus, so clients often came with a clear idea of what they wanted. To avoid the Pain Point of parking, they reached an agreement with a nearby car park to give their customers two hours free parking.

Since many of the customers, according to the Empathy Map, were passionate about gastronomy, they were invited to workshops to co-create dishes for the restaurant. In this way relationship experiences were produced. These co-creations were included on the menu with references like: "a suggestion from Alberto, Pedro or María". Thus, the menus were more fun and dynamic. Customers were able to boast about their creations and invited co-workers to try their own dishes at the restaurant. The menus were also changed, giving them a more modern design and larger font.

Since the restaurant was very spacious, they designed a section with partitions to offer greater privacy for business lunches and even job interviews in a more informal and personal environment. Tables were also fitted with plugs to connect laptops and other electronic devices.

Marcos also knew that it was essential to measure the experience of the client. He gradually implemented a series of indicators to determine how clients experienced their interactions with the restaurant. In this way, when clients were unhappy with something, the entire staff was involved in finding solutions quickly. They also analyzed the things clients rated highly when they recommended the restaurant to improve them even more.

On the last Friday of every month, they reserved the back room of the restaurant and invited a business leader or speaker to give a talk on negotiation, leadership, strategy, etc.

The clients also shared their own business experiences and there were all types of interesting events, such as wine tasting, presentations by brands of golf, padel or tennis equipment. And so, Marcos managed to make the restaurant not only a place for culinary experiences, but also a meeting point for business people interested in learning and exchanging ideas. The restaurant became a success by offering clients unique experiences and because of a firm belief in the Power of Customer Experience Strategy.

References:

- American Marketing Association
- Boston Consulting Group
- Carnegie, Dale (2008). Cómo ganar amigos e influir sobre las personas, Barcelona: ELIPSE
- Cepeda, I., & Ortega Gutierrez, J. (2020). La co-creacion de valor, y su influencia en los resultados empresariales en centros deportivos Cuadernos de Psi- cología del Deporte
- Curedale, Robert (2016) Experience Maps Journey Maps Service Blueprints Empathy Maps, Kindle Edition
- Customer Experience Professionals Association (CXPA)
- Drucker, Peter F (2003) Drucker esencial: Los desafíos de un mundo sin fronteras, Barcelona: Edhasa
- Ekman, Paul (2017) El Rostro de las Emociones, Barcelona: RBA Libros
- Enhancing emotion-based learning in decision-making under uncertainty D Alarcón, JG Amián, JA Sánchez-Medina - Psicothema, 2015
- Fitzgerald, Maurice & Fitzgerald, Peter (2017) Net Promoter Implement the System: Advice and Experience from Leading, Kindle Edition
- Gallup com
- Gartner com
- Gounaris, S P , Tzempelikos, N A , & Chatzipanagiotou, K (2007) The relationships of customer-perceived value, satisfaction, loyalty and behavioral intentions Journal of Relationship Marketing, 6(1), 63-87
- Goleman, Daniel (1996) Inteligencia Emocional, Barcelona: KAIROS
- Kahneman, Daniel (2013) Thinking, Fast and Slow, Kindle Edition
- Kotler, P , Linden, B , Stewart, A , & Armstrong, G (2001) Marketing, Australia: Prentice-Hall
- López Rosetti, Daniel (2018) Emoción y sentimientos: No somos seres racionales, somos seres emocionales que razonan, Barcelona: Ariel
- Mbango, P , & Toerien, D F (2019) The role of perceived value in promoting customer satisfaction: Antecedents and consequences Cogent Social Sciences, 5(1), 1684229

- Parasuraman, A , Zeithaml, V A , & Berry, L L (1988) Servqual: A multi- ple-item scale for measuring consumer perc Journal of retailing, 64(1), 12
- Pine, J , & Gilmore, J (1998) Welcome to the Experience Economy Harvard Business Review, 97-105
- Revella, A (2005) Buyer Personas: How to Gain Insight Into Your Customer's Expectations, Align Your Marketing Strategies, and Win More Business, Kindle Edition
- Schmitt, Bernd H (2014) Customer Experience Management, Kindle Edition
- Sirota, David (2005) El Empleado Entusiasta, Wharton School Publishing
- Zaltman, G (2003) How customers think: Essential insights into the mind of the market Harvard Business Press
- Zeithaml, V A , Berry, L L , & Parasuraman, A (1993) The nature and determinants of customer expectations of service Journal of the academy of Marketing Science, 21(1), 1-12

CARLOS CORREA RODRÍGUEZ

IT´S NOT MAGIC, IT´S CUSTOMER EXPERIENCE STRATEGY

KEY IDEAS TO APPLY
TO MY PROJECT FROM CHAPTER:

KEY IDEAS TO APPLY
TO MY PROJECT FROM CHAPTER:

KEY IDEAS TO APPLY
TO MY PROJECT FROM CHAPTER:

KEY IDEAS TO APPLY TO MY PROJECT FROM CHAPTER:

**KEY IDEAS TO APPLY
TO MY PROJECT FROM CHAPTER:**

KEY IDEAS TO APPLY
TO MY PROJECT FROM CHAPTER:

Printed in Great Britain
by Amazon